TRANSFORMING ENCOUNTERS WITH JESUS

(A current reflection on encounters found in the Gospel according to Saint Luke)

(Volume I)

Enrique Luis Ruloff

ediciones carolina

Transforming Encounters with Jesus

1° edition in Spanish June 2004

Translation to English by Sandra Robertson and Bryon Butler

Copyright 2005 by Enrique Luis Ruloff

Copyright 2005 by Ediciones Carolina

La Pampa 2975

(1428) Ciudad Autónoma de Buenos Aires

Tel. 54-11-4783-1127

E-mail elruloff@sion.com or enriqueruloff@hotmail.com

ISBN 9974-7906-3-8

Deposit made according to the law 11.723

Edited in Argentina

April 2005 by Enrique Luis Ruloff

Dedication

To all those whose names are not
recorded in any earthly book.
To all those whose histories and testimonies
have not been recorded nor remembered
To all those who never addressed
crowds at important conferences
To all those who in silence and
humility serve God faithfully
To all those who are anonymous, yet whose
names are written down in the Book of Life

Acknowledgements

Working on the project for a number of months has brought to mind all those who made this book possible. I deeply thank the following:

First, I am thankful to Jesus who, quietly and without fanfare, came into my life when I was a teenager. As well, I want to thank God the Father and the Holy Spirit for their gift of grace.

I want to thank my parents who guided me toward the gospel when I was young. I have never forgotten those Sunday mornings when my parents, my siblings and I, and my 90 year old great-grandmother traveled nine miles to church in a horse and wagon. I am reminded of those days whenever I see the TV show Little House on the Prairie.

I want to thank the church family in Puán, a small city in the province of Buenos Aires, Argentina. There my family and I had the opportunity to serve God and share the ideas that would eventually find their way into this book. We remember fondly the years we invested there, not only for the lives that God allowed us to impact, but for the love and impact we received as well.

I want to thank my family: my wife Paula and our five children: Jennifer, Jacqueline, Christopher, Stephanie and Nicole. God has given me the privilege of having a family that I yearn to return home to whenever I'm away. Thank you, Paula, for your selfless dedication; for postponing your dreams and investing these years in us. I am sure that one-day you will see flourish the fruits of your labor of love. I have, and continue, to rely on your unconditional support and I love you very much.

I want to thank the church family at our new church plant in Villa Urquiza, in Buenos Aires. It excites us to see the changes that God, gradually yet profoundly, is doing in the life of each member. Perhaps one day their stories, their transforming encounters with Jesus, will be written down.

I want to thank everyone who, in one way or another, has been an important part of this project, and whose imprint is on each page of this book. Without knowing it they have been an example in my life of what happens when people have transforming encounters with Jesus. I especially want to thank Bryan Buttler and Sandra Robertson for doing the translation to the English, Terry Bentley and Brian Plescher for helping me in the correction. Thanks as well go to Jaime Díaz for helping see this work come to print.

Prologue

Enrique Luis Ruloff is one of God's many anonymous believers in Argentina. He is a church planting pastor in Buenos Aires, and works as professor and for many years was the academic dean at the Buenos Aires Bible Institute, and finds time for his own "church", his wife Paula, and their five children. One can see God's blessing not only in his labors and in his family, but also in his solid testimony, his fidelity, and his integrity.

Now, in addition to his other ministries, he is benefiting us with this material, especially designed for use in cell groups. From the hands of a beautiful Christian, one of those special, anonymous, faithful, and upright believers that our Lord has in our blessed nation, comes an ideal book at an ideal time—a book for a country awakening to the need and value of the cell group experience. Coming from the pen of Enrique, this book is sure to be a blessing and help to your life and that of your congregation.

Alberto Eduardo Rizzo

Pastor of the Kyrios Christian Center en Villa Adelina, Buenos Aires, and coordinator of the Church Planting Masters Program at the Buenos Aires Biblical Institute

Contents

Dedication

Acknowledgments

Prologue

Contents

Introduction

Appetizer for the Soul I: The Drugstore

Chapter 1. The Calling of the Undesirables (Luke 5:1-11)

Study Guide

Questions for Study and Discussion

Appetizer for the Soul II: The Worm

Chapter 2. Touching the Untouchable (Luke 5:12-16)

Study Guide

Questions for Study and Discussion

Appetizer for the Soul III: The Other Woman

Chapter 3. God Reveals Himself (Luke 5:17-26)

Study Guide

Questions for Study and Discussion

Appetizer for the Soul IV: A true Christian

Chapter 4. Characters from a Real Story (Luke 5: 17-26)

Study Guide

Questions for Study and Discussion

Appetizer for the Soul V: The Treasure Hidden in the Land

Chapter 5. The Utmost Need (Luke 5:27-32)

Study Guide

Questions for Study and Discussion

Appetizer for the Soul VI: Puzzle

Chapter 6. Paralysis Versus Movement (Luke 6:6-11)

Study Guide

Questions for Study and Discussion

Appetizer for the Soul VII: White Roses

Chapter 7. From the Heights to the Depths (Luke 7:1-10)

Study Guide

Questions for Study and Discussion

Appetizer for the Soul VIII: The Barber

Chapter 8. Joyful Funeral Procession (Luke 7:11-17)

Study Guide

Questions for Study and Discussion

Appetizer for the Soul IX: God does not Sponsor Failures

Chapter 9. Spilling the Good to be Tilled with the Best

Study Guide

Questions for Study and Discussion

Appetizer for the Soul X: Roses for Valentine's day

Chapter 10. Defeated Giant (Luke 8:26-39)

Study Guide

Questions for Study and Discussion

Appetizer for the Soul XI: The Geese

Chapter 11. From Suffering to Happiness (Luke 8:40-42, 49-56)

Study Guide

Questions for Study and Discussion

Appetizer for the Soul XII: A Ring to my Mother

Chapter 12. Touching the Cloak of Salvation (Luke 8:43-48)

Study Guide

Questions for Study and Discussion

Appetizer for the Soul XIII: The Chinese Quarry Worker

Chapter 13. Feeding Many on Little (Luke 9:10-17

Study Guide

Questions for Study and Discussion

Conclusion

Bibliography

Introduction

✝

Michael is married and has a family, and some years back he and his wife became believers. If you were to know Michael now, if you were to sit and talk with him at one of Buenos Aires' many coffee shops, you would be surprised to learn how tragedy and violence marked his early years. Michael knew a life of suffering, beginning from the day of his birth. It was on that day that his mother died and his father turned his pain into a hatred for his son, blaming him for his wife's death. Wanting to be rid of him, Michael's dad sent him to his parents' home in the interior of Argentina. There he was raised, feeling like an unwanted nuisance to his grandparents. An uncle who also lived there began to physically abuse him, to the point where Michael needed to escape. When he was ten years old, with the help of some friends, he left the interior of Argentina and escaped to Buenos Aires, a world-class city of over 11 million people. Stepping down from the train, Michael was surprised to see a world far removed from the rural interior of the country, a new world with many buildings, cars and people. In Latin culture, family and friends mean everything, and even though his family situation was not healthy, though he often felt lonely, he was not alone. Stepping down from the train onto the sidewalks of an impersonal city, he began to feel both lonely and alone. He felt abandoned.

In Buenos Aires Michael made friends and lived with some garbage dump until one day an apparently friendly lady invited him to live with her in exchange for work. What he had hoped would be a better life turned into a nightmare, as he became a virtual work and sex slave to the woman. Eventually tiring of this misery, Michael left and returned to the streets, but no longer as an innocent child. He was now an adolescent matured beyond his years.

In the streets he met up with a gang and was forced to work for them, thus continuing the cycle of slavery that he had known. For many more months he continued to exist, a victim with neither hope nor home.

During this time he fell in love with the sister of one of the gang leaders. After some months they decided to live together, and not too long after their first child was born. Hoping to give his child a better life, Michael and his wife returned to the interior of the country. Setting up house in a small shack made of wood and tin, they hoped for the best, but Michael found no work and soon their money began to run out.

Driven to drink by the loss of hope, Michael became violent just like his uncle had been to him as a young boy. The loss of hope, the alcohol, the loneliness, frustration and helplessness led to more violence against his wife and small child, and each day took him deeper down a dead end street.

At last he found work in construction. One day at lunch a fellow worker, a young man named René, saw that Michael had nothing to eat. René shared his lunch with Michael, causing Michael to ask himself "What does this guy want with me?" as his life to that point had been filled with people who gave, only to take and cause him damage. Day after day Michael and René shared René's lunch. One day, Michael asked him what was different about him. Given this opportunity, René, a Christian, shared his testimony and invited Michael to go with him to church the following Sunday. At first Michael declined the invitation, as he did not believe he would be accepted there, although René encouraged him that he would be.

That Sunday, Michael did not go to church, but spent his time drinking. As the weeks passed he continued his downward spiral. He wanted to lead the type of life René lead, but his anguish, violent tendencies and frustration had made him a prisoner. Michael continued to decline the invitations that René extended to him.

One Sunday, as was his custom, Michael left home to drink, but on the way to the bar, he sensed that he should go visit René at church. Upon arriving, he was met by René and greeted by the congregation. Throughout the service Michael felt disoriented. The congregation sang a chorus little known to him, and the pastor preached a message related to the theme of the chorus: the love of God. It seemed to Michael that the entire service had been prepared especially for him. He thought, "Could it be that a God so big, who made the universe, could love me?"

At the end of the service, Michael asked to speak with the pastor. Patiently, the pastor answered the thousand and one questions that Michael asked. Finally, he fell to his knees near the front of the church, asked God to forgive him, and received Christ as his personal Savior. When he finally returned home late that evening, his wife was in bed pretending to sleep, afraid of her husband and his violent nature.

When Michael entered the bedroom, his child began to cry. He went to his cradle and raised his hand. His wife, fearful that her child was about to be hit again, tried not to look, but became spellbound at the site of her husband holding and rocking their child until he fell asleep.

Missionary and professor Jean Shannon in a Narrative Preaching class that we co-taught at the Buenos Aires Bible Institute told this true story. It is one of the millions of stories that could be told of men and women who have been transformed by the power of Jesus Christ.

The purpose of this book is to look at some of the transforming encounters that Jesus had with men and women during His earthly ministry in Israel. At the same time, we will highlight these encounters by relating modern transforming encounters, like that of Michael, and see how Christ can still change lives.

In the following pages we will be focusing on the transforming encounters found in the Gospel of Luke. Luke, a follower of Christ and a doctor, focused on the humanity of Christ and on the impact He made on the lives of those around Him. These encounters are presented in a contemporary way, that is to say, this book hopes to show that what these people experienced more than two thousand years ago is as relevant and fresh today as it was back then. Jesus is the same yesterday, today and forever.

Transforming Encounters with Jesus not only hopes to relate and "rediscover" those transforming moments from the Gospel of Luke, but to also make them a study tool for preaching or for personal and cell group Bible study. Due to the number of encounters included, they are divided into two parts. This book includes 13 of these encounters, a sufficient amount for a good three months of home Bible studies. Besides the narration or development of the story, at the end of each chapter the reader will find a brief outline summary, as well as questions to guide and facilitate a small group study for Christians or non-Christians. Finally, there are brief questions that will confront the reader personally with Biblical truth.

Our lives are a continual narration, and each day we are writing a chapter or chapter section. Each life is a special story that should be narrated and used to impact other lives. This is not to say that we should be submerged in desperation, anguish, and slavery or vice, in order to have an impacting life story. It is not just a dark or hidden past that can impact lives. It is Jesus who makes an impact through us. Like the prayer of Jabez, we need to ask God to bless our lives, to widen our sphere of influence, that His hand would be over us and that He would help us not to stumble. Each one of us has experienced the love of God, whether as a Christian or not, and if we would but stop for a few moments, we could write our own story. Each experience, small or big, that we have lived can be used to serve others. A human being is someone who lives and is sustained by stories. It has been said that no institution can survive if it renounces or does not capitalize on its story. Many believe, and with reason, that God loved our story so much that he was willing to make Himself a man in the Person of Jesus in order to be part of our story.

The transforming encounters with Jesus that we will read in the following pages have the objective not only to inform, but also to reach into your heart, to impact your own life and to provide elements and principles that will help you change your own life and allow it to impact the lives of others. I invite you to join me as we sojourn together through each of the following stories and experience together the transforming power of Jesus in our own story. As with any sojourn you will need to take the time to meditate, reflect and apply the spiritual truths that God wants to use to impact your own life...your own story. You will find this book easy to read, but I ask you not to read it quickly, but rather slowly and deliberately, because it is the seed that falls on good ground that will grow and bring forth abundant fruit. And so with this I welcome you to this journey, with the certainty that in the end you will not be the same person as you are now.

Appetizer for the Soul I

✝

The Pharmacy

There was not a worse job in the small, rural Argentine town than that of the doorman of a pharmacy, but what other job could he do? He had never learned to read or write, and had never done anything else. One day an enterprising young man, creative and restless, took charge of the pharmacy. He decided to modernize it, so he made a number of changes and called a meeting with the staff to give them new instructions. To the doorman he said "Beginning today, besides your position at the door, you are to prepare me a weekly report in which you will tell how many people come in every day, and will note any comments and recommendations they have regarding the service." The man shook with fear. He had always done his best, but this was too much for him. "I want to do a good job for you, he stammered, "but I don't know how to read or write" "I'm sorry then," said the manager, "but you will not be able to continue working here." "Please, sir, you can't fire me. I have worked this job my whole life." The manager stopped him. "Look, I understand" he said, but I can do nothing for you. I'll give you unemployment until you find other work. I'm sorry. Good luck." With that, he turned and left.

The man felt like his world had fallen apart. He never thought that he would find himself in this situation. What would he do? He thought about his time at the pharmacy. When a chair or table broke, he was always able to easily make a temporary repair. He thought that he could continue this type of carpentry work until another job came along. As he only had some rusty nails and a pair of dented pliers, he decided to use some of the unemployment money to purchase a set of tools. Since the town had no hardware store, he had to travel two days by mule to reach a town where he could buy what he needed. "What am I waiting for?" he thought, and set out to purchase his tools. When he returned, he brought with him a beautiful set of tools, and was ready to begin working.

Almost immediately, a neighbor came to his door. "I've come to ask if you had a hammer I could borrow." "Look", the man said, "I just bought one, but I need it to work, as I no longer am working at the pharmacy. I can lend it to you, but I need it back early tomorrow." The next morning, the neighbor brought it back and said "I am still not done, why not sell me the hammer?" "No", the man said, "I need it for my work, and the nearest hardware store is two days by mule." "Let's make a deal", the neighbor replied. "I will pay you the two days travel, and the price of the hammer, if you'll sell it to me." The man accepted and began another trek by mule to replace the hammer. Upon his return, another neighbor was at his door. "I need some tools." I'll pay you the four days travel, the price of the tools, and a small profit besides since I don't have the time to make the trip." With this, the ex-pharmacy doorman opened up his toolbox and sold a pair of tweezers, a screwdriver, a hammer and a chisel. He thought, "Certainly other people might need me to travel and buy them tools. I could even save travel time if I have a few customers at the same time." Soon more people from the neighborhood were coming to his door, and he had a small but growing clientele.

Once a week, the new tool troubadour traveled and purchased his clients requests. He rented a storehouse to store the tools, and a few weeks later, with a show window, the storehouse became the first hardware store in the town. Everyone was happy and bought their tools from him. As he was a good customer he no longer traveled; the tool-makers sent him what he needed. Over time, those in the neighboring villages began buying from him rather than traveling the two days to the other hardware store as they had before.

One day it occurred to him that his friend, a tool maker could make the hammer heads that he needed. And if he could make the hammerheads, he could probably also make the pliers, tweezers and the chisels. Later, he began making the nails and screws as well. To make a long story short, in ten years, the man, with honesty and hard work, was a millionaire tool-maker.

One day the man decided to donate a school to the town. There students could learn not only reading and writing, but also practical job skills. During the dedication ceremony the major gave the man the key of the city, hugged him and said "It is with great pride and gratitude that we ask you to give us the honor of writing your name on the first page in the first book of the new school." "The honor would be mine," said the man, "and nothing would give me more pleasure than to sign the book, but I don't know how to read nor write. I am illiterate." The mayor stood dumbfounded "You? You developed a million dollar industry without knowing how to read or write? I am astonished. I ask myself, 'what would you have been if you had known how to read or write?'"

"I can answer that" said the man calmly, "If I would have known how to read and write, I would have been a doorman at the pharmacy!"

Generally, changes are seen as adversities.   Yet adversities bring blessings. Crises are full of opportunities.   To change and to adapt oneself to the changes are always the best option.

God says "For I know the plans that I have for you" says the Lord, "plans to prosper you and not to harm you, to give you a future and a hope." (Jeremiah 29:11)1

Chapter One

†

The Calling of the Undesirables

One day as Jesus was standing by the Lake of Gennesaret,
with the people crowding around him and listening
to the word of God, he saw at the water's edge two boats,
left there by the fishermen, who were washing their nets.
He got into one of the boats, the one belonging to Simon,
and asked him to put out a little from shore. Then he
sat down and taught the people from the boat.

When he had finished speaking, he said to Simon,
«Put out into deep water, and let down the nets for a catch.»
Simon answered, «Master, we've worked hard all night
and haven't caught anything. But because you say so,
I will let down the nets.» When they had done so,
they caught such a large number of fish that their
nets began to break. So they signaled their partners in
the other boat to come and help them, and they
came and filled both boats so full that they began to sink.
When Simon Peter saw this, he fell at Jesus' knees and said,
«Go away from me, Lord; I am a sinful man!» For he and
all his companions were astonished at the catch of
fish they had taken, and so were James and John,
the sons of Zebedee, Simon's partners.

[1]Then Jesus said to Simon, «Don't be afraid; from now
on you will catch men.» So they pulled their boats up on shore,
left everything and followed him.

Luke 5:1-11 (See also Matthew 4:18-22 and Mark 1:16-20).

A true story is told about an alcoholic woman who one Sunday evening attended a church service and received Christ as Savior. A few days later one of the pastors went to visit her husband, an intelligent mechanic who was opposed to Christianity but devoted to other beliefs. He had been very unhappy with his wife's conversion, and told her that he had not doubt that she would soon return to her old ways.

Six months later the mechanic went to visit the pastor. He was very perplexed over his spiritual condition and said "I have read almost every book dealing with the evidences of Christianity, and have been able to resist their arguments, but in the last six months my wife's behavior is something that I can not refute. I have come to the conclusion that I must be mistaken, that Christianity must have holy and supernatural power, that it could take an alcoholic and make her a saint: an enchanting, sweet, patient and pious woman.

Certainly, the best books dealing with Christianity are transformed lives, lives that have responded to the call of God in Christ. As I write this chapter I am in the outskirts of Sao Pablo, Brazil, at a retreat for directors and deans of theological schools in the garden of the building. Each student at the seminary has his or her own story, his or her own experience in Christ Jesus.

One day after lunch a young woman who worked as a nutritionist told me her story. Her name was Yerusha Fernandes Pinto and she was 24 years old. One day, when she was four, due to the deaths of some close friends, her mother explained to her the plan of salvation. But it wasn't until she was seven that she understood what it meant to be a Christian.

One day while playing in the garden at her house she had a premonition, as if everyone had been snatched away and only she remained. There in the garden she recommitted her herself to Christ, giving him control of her life. At age 13, in front of a youth camp bonfire, she sensed that the Lord was calling her into ministry.

After another struggle in her faith, she recommitted herself, and at age 15 began ministering to hundreds at youth camps about the transforming power of Christ. She continued to grow in her Christian faith, and spent more time seeking God. When she was 18 years old, she enrolled in an intensive discipleship course at a seminary to help prepare her for university study. It was after this that her faith experienced another wilderness wandering. In the university she began to spend more time with a number of non-Christians and this lessened her devotion to God. As well, she saw that her church was doing little to meet the needs of these friends, and became frustrated and began losing the intimacy with God that she had had before. Yet during this time God dealt with her, and her sense of distance and loneliness and anguish led her to return to His care again.

In January of 2001 her parents helped her see that the time had come to recommit herself to Christ and remain firm in Him. Her days of playing with fire, of taking God's grace for granted, needed to end. Today, with hindsight, she can see more clearly her wilderness wanderings, and can understand better her own vulnerability. Her experiences have helped her to alter her vision of both the world and the church. She understands that the world is never able to satisfy the deepest needs of a person. Upon returning home after being with her college friends, she felt lonely. Now, she feels complete in Christ Jesus. When I asked her what Jesus means in her own life, she responded with tears "He is so merciful, and never tires of forgiving and giving someone a new beginning."

When we read the passages that deal with the calling of the first disciples we notice clearly that, if we were to look for people to begin a successful business, we never would have chosen people like those chosen by Christ. His disciples were the undesirables, not society's power players. Yet there was something that happened in the lives of these disciples that caused them to pass from anonymity to eternity. They become different people. When we, over 2000 years removed from these events, respond to God's calling, our lives as well can drastically change. When we read about the calling of the first disciples we notice four distinct stages.

Life before the Calling

Andrew, Peter, James and John were simple fishermen; to many they were of the economically lower class. We see from the Bible that they had a small fishing business, and earned a living by selling the fish they had caught the previous night. In those days there was no way to preserve their fish; they had to sell what they had just caught. They simply lived day by day, trusting God to supply their needs. They were humble fisherman that drew the attention of no one, who simply lived and worked. They were the owners of their own boats, and when Jesus approached them they were carrying out their tasks. They were responsible, dedicated to their fishing business with its fish, sales, boats and nets needing repairs— this was the world they knew. Perhaps their language was coarse, and their religious devotion was met once a year when they traveled to Jerusalem to make offerings and worship God.   For the most part their lives were tranquil and serene. They were of humble stock and, like many, were waiting for the Messiah, the one promised by the prophets in the Old Testament.   They recognized their sin, and maybe they were respectful to the contemporary prophet. Evidently they had heard Jesus speak before, or at least had heard of him.

When Jesus got in the boat and told Peter to throw the nets into the sea, Peter told him "We have fished all night and have not caught anything, but since you have asked me to throw over the nets I will do that." In other words, Peter was telling him "You understand your work very well, you know a lot about religion and things like this, but here I am the expert. However, since you have asked me to do this, I will." Another person might have insulted him, but the fact that Peter was in no way an intellectual did not mean he was disrespectful. Perhaps he obeyed the Lord to show him that there were no fish.

Jesus knows our lives, whether we be workers, students, housewives, masons, mechanics, executives, organizational leaders, fishermen or merchants. It might be that you are very comfortable with your life and can sympathize with religious questions, but in the depth of your heart you don't have peace. In light of this passage we see that it is not sufficient to merely accept that Jesus was a good teacher, as it won't make you into a son or daughter of God. It might be that you respect Christians, a priest, rabbi or pastor. Although commendable, this alone will not save you. Peter did not understand why a non-fisherman was now calling the shots, but nonetheless he obeyed him. Today there are many things we might not understand, but God wants us to trust Him.

The Calling

Upon seeing them, Jesus said "Follow me and I will make you fishers of men".   Here we have a great spiritual truth that we need to pay special attention to, whether we are Christians or not. To follow Jesus directly implies that we be fishers of men. If we are not reaching others with the gospel we should ask ourselves if we really are following the Christ of the Bible. It might be that we are following his teachings and doctrines as a philosophy of life. But true Christianity consists of following a person named Jesus and allowing that he live his life in us. This is one of the biggest differences between Christianity and other religions. Right now

Jesus calls you and says "Follow me and I will make you a fisher of men." He is saying "Come to me, repent of your sins, receive my forgiveness, receive me in your life as your personal Savior. Leave your old life behind and begin a new life, one that you can share with others."

Salvation is not an objective in itself. Salvation is a new reality freely offered by God in Christ to everyone who wants to receive it. But it is only a bridge to reach others. God does not want to save people just so they can be examples that others will be going to hell. God desires that each of his children share this calling that He shared with us to those who are lost, far from Him, without biblical faith and hope. One time, and with reason, someone once said "We should not ask God to add years to our lives, rather we should ask that he add life to our years." A Christian or church that does not share its faith with others is destined to stagnate. A Christian or church that does not share its faith is spiritually paralyzed.

I remember when both of my grandparents, due to poor health, could not move. My grandmother had to have her legs amputated, and my grandfather, due to blindness, spent most of his final years in bed. Due to these debilitations both suffered from bedsores. In the same manner, a believer or church that is paralyzed begins to experience spiritual bedsores and bodily pains. When a church stops growing outwardly, it will become inward focused and expend more energy on discussions, criticism and diversion, rather than following the heart of Christ. Yet God reconciled us to himself so that we can be agents of reconciliation for others. When we don't do it, we deny the reason for our existence.

The Answer

When Peter saw the miraculous catch of fish, he fell on his knees before Christ, convinced of his sins. Since he was an expert in his line of work he knew very well that what just happened was impossible. He could not resist such holiness, such power, in the same way the mechanic at the beginning of the chapter could not resist the changes that God had made in his wife. Peter responded to the Lord: "Master, we've worked hard all night and haven't caught anything. But because you say so, I will let down the nets." The astonishment and conviction of his sin seized him and the others, and they responded with conviction to the calling of Christ. The inevitable question that we must ask is "What will be your answer to this opportunity? Will you finish reading the chapter? Will you leave the book for another time? Or will you respond positively to Christ's call? Don't forget that right now, this moment, Christ is calling you. It is not by chance that you are reading about Christ and his transforming encounters.

These men were born again, they put Christ first in their lives, repented of their sins and accepted the forgiveness that Christ offered. In the same manner, Christ continues calling men and women today to follow Him and not religion. He does not want a halfhearted conversion from his followers. He wants us to receive him as Lord and dedicate ourselves to his interests, putting ours second.

I remember once hearing the story of an older man. He was a member of an evangelical church and had attended its services throughout his life, but his own spiritual life was sterile. Later, after he had dedicated himself fully to Christ, he said "I was accustomed to being comparatively pure, relatively honest, intermittently disinterested and generally caring." It should not surprise us that this type of Christianity produces halfhearted believers. Yet Jesus requires all or nothing. He does not want our possessions without our hearts. We need to remember that God does not need our offerings, our time, or our ethics. He does not want only a part of us. He wants all of us. It is not difficult to find many frustrated Christians today, Christians who decide to live a halfhearted spiritual life, with one foot in the church and the other in the world.

The famous missionary to China, Hudson Taylor, once said: "When Christ came to the world, the first thing he did was empty himself of His glory so that he could fill us with his Grace. " He gave all that he possessed, even his own life. Thus we, as a prerequisite of filling others, must empty ourselves of honor, status, and opportunities. In Christianity this renouncing gives us the blessings to enrich others. This is just what the first disciples of Jesus did; they left everything and followed Him. Why do we find Christians full of rancor, frustration, criticism, hurts and bitterness? We find this simply because they have not emptied themselves so that Christ can fill them with his grace. Therefore, what they do offer is the bitterness, resentment, etc., that is inside of them. Dear reader, God does not want this for you. He wants to fill us each day with his Holy Spirit, to be manifest in us as He was manifest in the life of the apostle Paul in Ephesians 5:18, which is similar to how he ends each of his letters. Every believer needs to grow daily in the grace of God. It is not a static measuring. Peter, when writing his second letter, says in chapter 3:18 "But grow in the grace and knowledge of our Lord and Savior Jesus Christ. To him be glory both now and forever! Amen." Today, more than ever, the church of Christ needs men and women full of grace, able to love and forgive those that waste their spiritual inheritance by living far from Christ, but who want to return to Him.

The results

The results were many and abundant. They began a time of transformation, knew Christ as Savior and, in spite of their failings, defeats and spiritual frustrations, came to be great preachers of the Gospel, to the point that they were considered worthy of martyrdom for the cause of Christ. They had become fishers of men.

It is possible that God does not want you to leave your family, home, work and responsibilities to go preach the Gospel across the seas. He is hoping that you will be a fisher of men where you are. There are many Christians who weep for the lost in other countries yet don't care while there neighbors, family, friends and fellow workers are walking the road to hell. If someone is not willing to reach the lost in their own area, there is not guarantee that they could do it in another country.

One time a missionary asked a Chinese man if he had heard the Gospel. He replied that he had not heard it, but he had seen it. He said, "I know a man who terrorized our district, a person so bad, so lost that he was almost a savage. And, he smoked opium. When he accepted the religion of Jesus, he changed radically, so much so that he is the most gentle, the best of men, and has been able to abandon his terrible vices. Yes, I can say that I have not heard the gospel, but I have seen it."

The apostle Paul, writing to the Corinthians, tells them that we are an open letter of the Gospel. A well-known yet timely phrase says "Your life speaks so loudly that I cannot hear your words." Our lives are open letters. Many people, both believers and non-believers, observe us, looking to see if we are congruent in what we believe and how we live.

A true encounter with Jesus Christ is a transforming encounter. It changes us inside and out, making us new, even affecting the simple things in our lives. If Jesus is not continually changing us, even though we have been believers for many years, perhaps it is because we have grown lukewarm.

A milkman who regularly watered down milk became a Christian. Everyone was able to see the difference, not only in a life transformed, but also in milk that tasted differently! One lady, who regularly bought his milk and had known him a long time, asked one day if he was using better cows or better pastures. "No madam", answered the milkman, "I have the same cows, and the same pastures, the milk is better because I became a believer in Jesus Christ, which made the milk better, too!" These are the fruits of a true Christian conversion.

When Christ transforms us, he also changes aspects of our work, study, family relations, etc. Michael, who we met at the beginning of the book, experienced this transformation. If you, dear reader, have not experienced this spiritual transformation, a transformation so real in the lives of his disciples, I encourage you to invite Jesus to enter your life. Give it to him completely, and you will experience this transformation. It does not matter how your life has looked to others, to God your life is worth a great price, an eternal price; the price of blood. Please do not despise a love so great. Allow the Holy Spirit to live in you and equip you to be a fisher of men; a life He wants for all of His children.

Study Guide

Introduction

Relate the story of the alcoholic woman and the conversion of her mechanic husband.

Transitional Phrase

The greatest books about Christianity are the transformed lives of those who have responded to the call of God in Jesus Christ.

Bible reading

Matthew 4:18-22; Mark 1:16-20 and Luke 5:1-11. These passages show us four important things

1. Life before the Calling

Briefly review the lives of Peter, Andrew, James and John. Give the historical framework, their responsibilities, and the frustration of a fruitless night of fishing. Talk about the arrival of Jesus and the challenge to toss the nets overboard one more time.

Application: Jesus knows all about your real life, whatever your work or social status. To sympathize with Christianity, to support it, is not enough. You must know Jesus as Savior.

2. The Calling

Spiritual Truth. To be a follow of Jesus means to be a fisher of men. Christianity consists of following a person named Jesus and sharing this faith with others. Someone has said: "We should not ask God to add years to our lives, but life to our years."

3. The Answer

Peter fell to his knees and recognized that Christ was Lord. The old man in the church, the one who had lived for years as a frustrated Christian, did the same. The spiritual truth is that we need to empty ourselves so that Jesus will fill us with his Glory and use us.

4. The Results

The disciples began a new phase, one of transformation. As the Chinese gentleman said, the gospel is not only heard, but seen as well.

Conclusion

Tell the story of the milkman who regularly watered down his milk and the resulting work that Christ did in his life. Today Christ can change your life, if you are open to hearing His call.

Questions for study and discussion

1. How can we define the conversion of a person to Christianity?

2. What is the difference between conversion and new birth?

3. How were the lives of the disciples before they knew Jesus? What type of work did Andrew, Peter, James and John do?

4. What indications does the passage give that they might have heard about Jesus before he approached their boat?

5. What was Jesus' challenge in relating to these people?

6. How did Jesus´ call them?

7. What was Peter's first reaction when he saw the miraculous catch of fish?

9. What was the first thing that the disciples did after hauling in the big catch of fish?

10. What were some of the immediate results of obeying this calling?

11. What were the long-term results of this obedience?

Applicational Activities

1. How would you describe your own conversion or new birth? What was your life like before you knew Christ as Savior?

2. What did Christ do to cause you to want to yield to Him?

3. What were some of the results that you experienced after becoming a believer?

4. Have you become a fisher of men? How many people have come to the Lord through your ministry?

Appetizer for the Soul II

†

The Worm

One day a small grasshopper crawled towards the sun. Along the way he encountered a grasshopper. "Where are you going?" the grasshopper asked. Without stopping, the caterpillar answered "Last night I had a dream; I dreamed that at the top of a great mountain I could see the whole valley. I loved the dream so much I decided to make it happen."

Surprised by his determined friend, the grasshopper said: "You must be crazy! How could a small caterpillar like you make it there? For you, a small stone would be a mountain; a small puddle a sea and a tree trunk an insurmountable barrier." Yet by this time the caterpillar was a ways away and did not hear the caterpillar's comments. His tiny little legs never stopped moving.

The caterpillar continued on his way, inch by inch. Meanwhile, a spider, a mole, a frog and a flower counseled the little guy to stop his madness. "You'll never make it!" they said. But inside, the caterpillar was living a dream that would not die.

Worn out, without strength and about to die, he decided to stop and rest, and with his last bit of strength he built a place to spend the night. "I'll be better soon", he said, and then he died. All of the animals in the valley came to look upon his remains. There lay the craziest animal (is a caterpillar an animal?) in town. As a tomb he had built a monument around himself, it reminded all of the others of the one who had died trying to live an impossible dream.

One morning when the sun was shining bright, all of the animals around the tomb were reminded of the foolishness of the dream. Soon they were astonished. The cocoon began to break, and with their own eyes they saw an antenna pop out. Little by little, as if to give them time to absorb the shock, they saw in front of them not a foolish caterpillar, but beautiful wings the color of a rainbow: **a butterfly.**

There was nothing to say. They all knew what he would do. He would fly towards the great mountain and make his dream come true; the dream for which he died and for which he was reborn.

They were all wrong. God would not have given us the possibility to dream, if he had not given us the opportunity to make those dreams come true. If you have a dream, live for it, live to reach it, live your life for it; and if you can't, perhaps you need to change.

Life's success comes not in what is gained, but in the obstacles that are met and overcome. Fight for what you believe in and you will live your dreams. Don't be disheartened if you have to try again and again; just keep trying.2

Something that has deeply impacted my life goes like this: "Those dreams that we dream in prayer are not only dreams." If God has given you a vision, pursue it until you reach it, you and those who come along after you.

Chapter Two

✝

Touching the untouchable

In one of the villages, Jesus met a man with an advanced
case of leprosy. When the man saw Jesus, he fell to the ground,
face down in the dust, begging to be healed. "Lord", he said,
"If you want to, you can make me well again".
Jesus reached out and touched the man. "I want to", he said.
"Be healed". And instantly the leprosy disappeared.
Then Jesus instructed him not to tell anyone what had
happened. He said, "Go right to the priest and let him
examine you. Take along the offering requiered in the
law of Moses for those who have been healed of leprosy,
so everyone will have proof of your healing.
Yet despite Jesus'instructions, the report of his power
spread even faster, and wast vrowds came to hear Him preach
and to be healed of their deseases. But Jesus often
withdrew to the wilderness for prayer.
Luke 5:12-16. (See also Matthew 8:2-4 and Mark 1:40-44).

Some years ago in a New York magazine there appeared a teachable statistic relating to two North American families. It analyzed the family of a Max Jukes, who did not believe in Christianity. He had married an atheist like himself. After a careful study of his family tree, which stopped when the article was published, it discovered that there were 1,026 descendents. Three hundred of them died young. One hundred were jailed for various reasons. One hundred and nine became protagonists of vice, living for carnal pleasure. One hundred and two were regular drinkers. In total, this particular family tree had cost the state of New York a sum total of $1,100,000.

The study also looked at the life of Jonathan Edwards, who as a Christian had married a young Christian believer who shared his spiritual convictions. Out of their union came 729 descendents, until the time of the study. Three hundred had been preachers, 65 had been professors in different universities, 13 had been university presidents, six were authors of quality books, three were congressmen and one was a United States Vice-President. Edward's lineage had not cost the State of New York one dollar; even better, his lineage had greatly impacted not only the United States, but the world as well.

It is known by all that sin separates us from God and produces not one good thing. The book of Luke tells us the story of the man destroyed, separated from society, who, when transformed by Jesus became a blessing. In the story we see that Jesus touched an untouchable. This story teaches that He also is available to touch our lives, no matter how dirty or destroyed by sin. The parallel passages in Matthew 8:2-4 and Mark 1:40-44 also narrate the same story more generally.

In Palestine there were two types of leprosy. One appeared as a skin disease, and although it was severe it was the least severe of the two. The more severe type began as a discoloration and continued growing until it began eating the skin, until the unfortunate person remained with only a stump of his or her arm or leg. It was literally a living death. Leviticus 13 and 14 contain the religious rules for cleanliness, with respect to leprosy. One with the more severe type of the disease remained isolated and had to cry out "unclean" when someone approached, where ever they might be. He had to live alone, away from the community. The person was no longer a part of community life and remained exiled. The result was, and is, that the psychological consequences of leprosy were and are worse than the physical ones.

A doctor in charge of a leper colony once said: "A leper is sick in both body and mind. For some reason leprosy has attached to it an attitude that causes it to seem different than other disfiguring diseases. It is associated with shame and horror, and it brings with it, in a mysterious way, a sense of guilt, even though the victim doesn't choose it; it chooses him." Separated from and hated by others, many times the leper will take his own life. He or she has been rejected by so many others that finally he begins to reject himself.

Leprosy begins when, for some reason, the flesh no longer feels pain, and feeling pain is often what allows one to remove himself from harm, and to survive. This is the type of man who came to Jesus; a filthy person that Jesus reached out and touched. And here we are confronted with a great pearl of spiritual wisdom, a great heavenly truth. Christ touched an un-touchable. The hands of Jesus, full of compassion, opened up to bring relief to a man all others had marginalized.

Many times a person's sin has been compared with leprosy, that it produces consequences similar in those who practice and are enslaved to it. The truths that we can draw from this disease and relate to sin are striking. Next we will look at a few of them.

Corruption

In the same way that leprosy corrupts human flesh, sin works to slowly corrupt the spirit of a person, until it ends up being a stump impenetrable to all, even to the grace of God. It works to slowly destroy the image of God in a person. As a leper no longer feels pain and slowly has his flesh destroyed, so the sinner, once he becomes immune to what sin is doing, is also destroyed.

There is a true story of a painter who painted a picture representing the innocence of man, using as a model a child named Rupert, who is praying on his knees with his mother. The palms of his hands are closed together, his rosy cheeks show his good health, while his blue eyes express devotion and peace. The artist was so satisfied with his work that he hung it in his studio.

A number of years later the artist, then old, wanted to paint a portrait dealing with the theme of "The Crime". Looking for a subject, he visited a jail and in a humble jail cell came upon a criminal named Randall. He was fastened in chains, his body wasted, his cheeks pale, and his eyes reflected anguish and vice. Asking permission to take him to his studio as a model, they left with a guard.

The prisoner was very happy, as this stranger, by chance, had lifted him from the squalor and monotony that was his life. Suddenly he fixed his eyes on the portrait that the painter had painted so many years before, and it dawned on him who the woman was who was holding the hands of the young child, a child of innocence and naïveté. At once he began to cry.

The painter stopped painting for a moment and asked the prisoner the reason for his grief. Pointing to the woman in the picture, the man said "That is my mother! I was that innocent child that you painted all those years ago. Sin and vice have made me the man I am now."

In the same way sin works its way in our lives. We slowly lose innocence, we become numb to its effects, until sin finally destroys us, corrupting and making bitter our existence. Sin, like leprosy, corrupts a person physically, mentally and spiritually.

Separation

As leprosy separated the leper from society, such that he or she had to live literally outside of society, sin separates us from God, from ourselves, from nature and from our neighbor. When we read in the book of Genesis the fall of Adam and Eve, we see that their sin produced this quadruple separation. First, it broke their relationship with God. When He visited them in the garden, as was His custom, the Bible account says that Adam and Eve hid themselves as they knew that they had done something prohibited. Second, there was a separation from themselves. The Bible says that they were naked and felt shame; previous to the call, they were naked but felt no shame. In the third and fourth place there was a separation between them and nature. Adam was guilty to Eve and Eve to the serpent.

When a brother or sister are in sin, they generally do not dwell in the camp of the Lord, that is, they do not frequent church, but are outside of it both physically and spiritually. And while they might by cleansed by the grace of God they do not feel accepted by others. God said "It is your sins that separate you from God when you try to worship him" (Isaiah 59:2)

Shame

Verse 12 of the Biblical account tells us that the leper "when he saw Jesus, he threw himself down and begged him". So much was the shame that he felt that he could not even raise his head. His self esteem was very low. As his infirmity caused such shame and horror, in a similar way sin can cause shame and fear in a person. When Adam and Eve disobeyed, the first feelings that came to the surface were shame and fear as they realized they were naked and that God had come to visit them. Due to this, often when a Christian is far from God, it is hard to return to Him because he feels shame, that he has disappointed the Lord. This was the experience of Peter after he had denied Jesus. The biblical account tells us that after this denial, after his heart rendering tears, he returned to his former job as fisherman.

On one occasion I called the husband of a family in our congregation that was away from the church. I wanted to know how they were. We talked over the matter and, in any case, they decided not to return to our church family. He told me that he could not return after what had happened. His problem was that he felt shame as he had broken confidence. People like this, as well as many others far from God, need compassion, abundant grace and much patience to be reestablished in the body of Christ, which is the church.

With a great deal of passion, Peter had committed himself to following Jesus, and the shame of his denials had led him to leave what God had called him to. But Jesus, full of love and grace decided to reincorporate him, and Peter became what Jesus said he would be: a pillar in the church.

Guilt

As leprosy produces in its victims feelings of guilt, in the same way sin robs a person of mental and spiritual peace, submerging them in feelings of guilt. Sin enslaves us as Satan is a hard taskmaster, merciless, who charges high interest for the license that we take to sin. Yet confession and honest repentance brings liberation to a soul oppressed by sin. Jesus promised us that if we knew the truth it would set us free.

One time I heard the story of a lady who had white swimming ducks, of which some had won local contests which made the lady very proud. One day John, her young son, was trying out marksmanship with his new sling shot and wanted to see how close he could shoot to the ducks, as he had seen marksmen on their knees at the circus that had come to town. As guessed, John was not as good as he had hoped, and mortally wounded his mother's favorite duck, the very won that had won the competition the year before. Trying to hide his victim under a pile of hay, his sister came by and asked what he was doing. Forced to tell her the truth, she promised not to divulge what had happened.

His worry and anxiety over the incident robbed him of his appetite, nor would it allow him to sleep in peace. Every time that his sister was called upon to do the dishes after dinner she would say "John will help me." He protested, but she would quietly say to him "Remember the duck…." For some days he was a slave to the whims of his sister.

One day, tired of the situation, he approached his mother and confessed what had happened. He put his head in his mother's knees and sobbed, telling her he felt awful about what had happened. His mother said: "It hurts that you killed my favorite duck, but I am proud to have a son who knows how to confess the truth. " John told her: "Do to me what you want, but I felt so guilty that I had to confess what I had done." "I won't punish you," said his mother, "you have been punished enough during the time you tried to hide your guilt, I forgive you." Putting her arm around his neck, she kissed him.

That night, when his sister wanted to blackmail him to wash the dishes, John said to her: "Today I am going to do my own chores, mom knows what happened and has forgiven me."

And thus the child was freed from his slavery to sin; his confession and the forgiveness of his mother had brought liberation. In the same way, the devil endeavors to enslave us by sin with feelings of guilt and cruel blackmail. Yet as soon as we come to the Savior and confess to Him our guilt, we will find ourselves freed from the chains of the devil.

Death

Leprosy eventually causes death, as does sin. God says in His word that "For the wage of sin is death", yet He extends his hand to save us. He adds "But the free gift of God is eternal life through Christ Jesus our Lord" (Romans 6:23)

If we, like the leper, approach Jesus and say to Him "Lord, if you want to, you can make me well again", without a doubt Christ will say "I want to, be healed". He will touch our lives, our dirty, untouchable lives of corruption, shame, fear and death and will restore us to his house, will return to us a sense of the life He desires, and will fill us with His peace.

The psychological process of sin is double. First, when we reject ourselves, when our hearts are full of bitterness and shame, we should remember that, in spite of it all, the hand of Jesus is still extended towards us. It was Max Rutherford who wanted to add a new Beatitude when he said: "The beatitudes are what heal us from our rejection of ourselves". This is what Jesus did with the leper and what he wants to do with each person that finds themselves sick with the leprosy of sin. Second, to touch the untouchable, to love the one whom nobody loves, to forgive that which no one wants to forgive, is the essence of Christianity. Jesus did this, and so must we. While possibly the whole world hates those responsible for the attacks of September 11th, God's children are called to love them. In Jesus' day the Samaritans where rejected, yet Jesus defied what was expected and loved them. Therefore, it should not surprise us too much when the marginalized of a society, those without homes, the physically and socially sick, when these people come to know Christ. It was for the sick that Jesus came. It was high society that was invited to the feast in the biblical parable of the Great Banquet, but it was society's outcasts that actually participated in it.

After Jesus healed the leper, he told him to go to the priest in order to present an offering of thanks for his purification, which is what Moses had ordained, so that this would serve as a testimony. In the same way, when Jesus cleans us, we need to share our testimony so that others can share in our joy and worship God. What's more, the biblical narrative tells us that Jesus became famous throughout the streets of Israel. In the measure that we tell others what Christ has done for us, his fame will grow and many will seek Him in search of help.

We must not allow sin to destroy our lives as well as the lives of our children. If it is necessary, we must approach God and say to Him " Lord, if you want to cleanse me, please do it now." Without a doubt, He will extend his strong hands and with compassion will touch us and will say to us: "I want to, be clean." What is untouchable for a human being is what pleases God to touch and restore. He rejoices in finding pearls in a garbage dump.

Study Guide

Introduction

Relate briefly the results of the famous comparative study of the Jukes and Edwards families.

Transitional Phrase

Sin does not produce anything good, yet we will see the life experience of a man who suffered an untouchable disease. Nevertheless, Jesus touched and healed him.

Bible reading

Matthew 8:2-4; Mark 1:40-44 and Luke 5:12-16.

In this biblical account we can see five important things that the leprosy of sin produces in our lives.

1. Corruption

As leprosy corrupts the flesh, sin corrupts the spirit of a person. Briefly relate the story of the painter and his two works of art.

2. Separation

Leprosy separated the sufferer from society. Sin does the same thing: it separates us from God, from ourselves, from our neighbor and from nature.

3. Shame

The leper fell on his knees with his face to the ground. He was ashamed of his situation. In a similar way, when a person is living in sin and knows it, he feels ashamed before his Christian brothers and sisters. Adam and Eve, due to their shame, covered their bodies with leaves.

4. Guilt

The leper was made a prisoner of his guilt. In those days it was generally thought that leprosy was a curse for one's sins. Briefly tell the story of John, the child who killed his mother's favorite duck.

5. Death

Finally, leprosy kills a person. Eventually, sin will do the same in the life of a person; it will lead one to spiritual death. The only way to be free from this death is through Jesus Christ.

Conclusion

Healing produced gratitude in the leper and renown to Jesus. Our testimony can do the same.

Questions for study and discussion

1. Where was Jesus when he came upon the leper?

2. In those days, what did society think of leprosy and the leper?

3. Where did the leper live in the days of Jesus?

4. Why did the leper fall on his knees before Jesus? Think of some different motives.

5. What did the leper ask Jesus to do?

6. What was Jesus' answer, and what does this answer mean for us?

7. What are the similarities between leprosy and sin? List some of the consequences.

8. Why did Jesus tell the leper to present an offering of purification?

9. What were some of the results of this healing?

10. Why do you think that Jesus frequently withdrew to pray and be alone?

Applicational Activities

1. Have you personally experienced the cleansing of your sins by Jesus? Briefly tell your story.

2. How and in what areas of your life has the leprosy of sin affected you?

3. What practical steps have you, or could you take to keep yourself spiritually clean?

4. With how many people have you recently shared the good news of what Jesus can do?

Appetizer for the Soul III

†

The Other Woman

After 21 years of marriage, I discovered a new way to mantain the sparks of love with my wife. Not too long ago I decided to have an affair. Actually, it was my wife's idea.

"You know that you love her", she told me one day, taking me by surprise. "Life is too short, you should spend some time with her." "But I love you", I protested. "I know" she responded. "But you also love her."

The other woman, the one my wife went on about, was my mother, who had been widowed for going on 19 years. Yet the demands of my job and my three kids allowed me to visit her only occasionally. That night I called her to invite her to dinner and to the movies.

"What has happened? Are you all right" she asked me. My mother is the type of woman who thinks that a late night call or a surprise invitation indicates bad news. "I think it would be nice to spend some time with you" I said. "Just us." She thought a moment, and then said "I would like that a lot."

That Friday, while I drove to pick her up after work, I found myself feeling nervous. It was a nervousness reserved for a date. And, dear God! When I arrived to her house, I noticed that she too was moved by our date. I waited at the door and had her jacket ready. She had fixed her hair and was dressed in the dress she had used for her last wedding anniversary. She smiled and shined like an angel.

I told my friends that I was going to go out with my son, and they were very impressed, she said as she got into the car. "They can't wait until tomorrow to hear about our evening together."

We went to a cozy restaurant that was not too elegant, and my mother clung to my arm as if she were the first lady. When we sat down, I had to read her the menu, as her eyes could not catch the print. During the meal (?) I raised my eyes and saw that my mother was seated on the other side of the table and was looking at me. A nostalgic smile was on her face. "There was a time when I read the menu to you." She said. "Then it's time that you allowed me to return the favor." I responded.

During the dinner we enjoyed a pleasant, conversation; nothing extraordinary, simply sharing about our day and our lives. We talked so much that we missed the movie. "I'll go with you another time" said my mother when I dropped her off, "but only if you let me do the inviting."

"How was your date?" asked my wife when I got home that night. " Very pleasant, much more pleasant than I had thought." I responded. A few days later, my mother died of a massive heart attack. It happened so fast that there was nothing anyone could do. A few days later I received an envelope with a copy of a check of the restaurant where my mother and I had dinner and a letter that said: "I paid our dinner in advance. I was almost sure that I wouldn't be able to go, but I paid a dinner for two persons: your wife and you. You will never know what that night meant to me. I love you." In that moment I understood the importance of the words "I love you"; of giving to our loved ones the space that they deserve. Nothing in life is more important than God and one's family. Give them your time because they should not have to wait. The Bible says "Honor you father and your mother". *(Matthew 19:19)3*

Chapter Three

†

God Reveals Himself

One day while Jesus was teaching, some Pharisees and teachers
of religious law were sitting nearby. (It seemed that these men
showed up from every village in all Galilee and Judea, as well
as from Jerusalen). And the Lord's healing power was
strongly with Jesus. Some men came carring a paralyzed man
on a sleeping mat. They tried to push through the crowd to Jesus,
but they couldn't reach him. So they went up to the roof,
took off some tiles, and lowered the sick man down into
the crowd, still on his mat, right in front of Jesus. Seeing
their faith, Jesus said to the man, "Son, your sins are forgiven".
"Who does this man think he is?" the Pharisees and teachers
of religious law said to each other. "This is blasphemy!
Who but God can forgive sins?". Jesus knew what they were
Thinking, so he asked them, "Why do you think this is
Blasphemy?. It is easier to say, 'Your sins are forgiven' or
'Get up and wald'. I will prove that I, the Son of Man, have
the authority on earth to forgive sins". Then Jesus turned to
the paralyzed man and said, "Stand up, take your mat,
and go on home, because you are healed". And inmediately,
as everyone watched, the man jumped to his feet, picked up
his mat, and went home prising God. Everyone was gripped
whit great wonder and awe. And they praised God, saying
over and over again, "We have seen amazing things today".
Luke 5:17-26 (See also Matthew 9:2-9 and Mark 2:3-12).

It is told that one time Joseph Smith, the founder of the Mormon religion, took a group of his fanatic followers to a river, promising them that they would see him walk across the river without getting wet. When they arrived at the river, Smith asked them "Do you have faith that I can do this?" The enthusiastic followers responded "Yes, we have faith! We have faith!" "Good", said Joseph Smith, "then it is not necessary that I do this miracle." With that, they returned from where they had come.

At a certain moment in his ministry, Jesus said "Blessed are those that do not see yet believe." Nevertheless, He performed many miracles during his earthly ministry, explaining "The works that I do, they give testimony of me." Christ still works miracles in our lives, thus we can experience his divinity. Paul said, writing to the Romans "And Jesus Christ our Lord was shown to be the Son of God when God powerfully raised him from the dead by means of the Holy Spirit" (Romans 1:4). Only when we experience the change and power of Jesus Christ in our lives are we convinced of his divinity. And this is basically what this passage of Luke deals with in the healing of the paralytic. The central theme is to demonstrate to the hearers and listeners that Jesus is God.

It is said that faith moves mountains. The truth is that when we have an encounter of faith with Jesus, we discover some truths that lead us to other results. The four friends of the paralytic, when going to Jesus, were met with various surprises.

They discovered His power to heal

Luke says "The power of the Lord was present for Jesus to heal the sick" vs. 17). What power? The same power that Christ has received from God the day he was baptized, when the heavens opened and the Holy Spirit descended in the form of a dove; the same power that he first exhibited in the desert when he was tempted by the devil, and later when he entered the synagogue, opened the book of Isaiah and read the passage that says "the Spirit of the Lord is upon me, because He has chosen me to bring good news to the poor. He has sent me to proclaim liberty to the captives and recovery of sight to the blind, to set free the oppressed and announce that the time has come when the Lord will save his people" (Luke 4:18-20).

The Jesus who traveled the many dust covered trails of Israel has not changed. The same Holy Spirit enables him to work miracles today. He is the same yesterday, today and forever. One time, Dr. A.B. Simpson, the founder of the Christian and Missionary Alliance, was asked what his opinion was on divine healing. He answered "The question we must answer is not the one you asked, rather 'what is Christ's opinion?'" Without a doubt, part of his answer was accurate. If we today continue questioning or doubting if Jesus can or cannot do miracles, I believe that we still do not know Christ in abundance, or at least, we don't know the Christ the Bible shows us. It is less difficult for Christ to do a miracle of healing than to forgive our sins and give us a new heart.

The paralytic and his friends understood this truth. They knew and believed that the power of the Lord was with Jesus to heal. It was for this reason they approached him and did not allow obstacles to impede them in getting what they wanted. The houses of that time were vastly different from what we know to be houses today. They were made of brick or clay, and did not have roofs of metal or tile, but rather were of a type of terrace which were accessible via an outdoor stairway. What these four friends did was climb to this terraced roof by the stairway. They removed a part of the clay roof, along with some bricks, and with this created a hole through which they lowered the paralytic on his stretcher.

What is interesting is that his miraculous act resulted more from the faith of his four friends than it did from the paralytic; Jesus saw their faith, and not just that of the paralytic. What does this spiritual truth teach us? Simply, if we believe that Jesus is able to change people, then we should be bringing the paralytics in our society to the feet of Jesus; and not only physical paralytics, but also emotional, spiritual and psychological paralytics. That is to say, we can take to Jesus all those that need him. Why is it that many times Christians prefer to take relatively healthy people to church and not those considered problematic? Is it not that in the depths of who we are, it challenges us to believe that Jesus has the power to change an ill person?

We need to learn from these four friends and share with our needy communities a Christ who has the power to transform. They need to know that Jesus is able to help them, is able to heal and save them, that the power of God is in Christ to save and heal the sick. These four friends, together with the paralytic, discovered the power of Jesus to heal when they approached him in faith.

They discovered his Omnipresence

These friends not only discovered the power of Jesus to heal, but they also found someone who knew the thoughts of men. They met someone who did not miss a thing. As you read this, perhaps you have doubts in your heart or mind. Allow me to remind you that Jesus knows exactly what is inside each of our hearts. He knows how much faith we have or if we have it at all. Therefore, we should not approach him pretending to have enormous faith, but simply go to him without evasion and simply say to him "Lord, help my unbelief, I need to believe you and I want to believe you. Help me to recognize that in me are doubts, arguments, prejudices, but I need and want to believe you, help me." If your desire is sincere, without doubt Jesus will be there helping you in your weakness.

Perhaps you have attended meetings where a preacher prayed for sick people and they were healed. Maybe you yourself have prayed for someone and they weren't healed and you have asked "What does he have that I don't?" The answer is very simple: These people believed in the power and in the Word of God. They believed that Jesus still does miracles today as He did almost 2000 years ago. Do we believe that the Bible is the Word of God? Generally we admit that it is, but on the other hand it challenges us to believe it.

These four friends and the paralytic went in search of health, that is, the bread and the fish. They discovered that Jesus not only had the power to heal, but also knew the thoughts of men. They discovered that this simple carpenter of Nazareth could also read their minds and hearts.

They discovered his Divinity

At the heart of this passage is the divinity of Jesus. What Luke wanted to do when relating this episode is that the hearers and readers would discover and know that Jesus is also God. The argument of the Scribes and Pharisees was valid, that only God is able to forgive sins and no one else. The truth is that only God can forgive sins and there is no other intermediary or representative between God and man except Jesus. Now, if only God can forgive sins and Jesus did it, what does this show us? It shows us that Jesus is also God and that there is no difference between him and the Father. At another time Jesus pointed out "I and the Father are one." In this passage we find an important ordering of priorities. The friends brought the paralytic so that Jesus would heal him, yet Jesus did something different. He forgave his sins and later said "I tell you, get up, pick up your bed, and go home". Here there are two important things to take into account.

First, God wants to forgive us of our sins, of those things that separate us from Him. It serves nothing if we have all our body parts and yet spend eternity away from God. It is better, teaches Jesus, to lose a hand, a foot or an eye and go to heaven. Christ continues to have the power to heal, yet he is interested first in forgiving our sins, and removing those things that separate us from God.

Second, there is an intimate relation between sickness and sin. I am not saying that all sickness is the consequence of some specific sin that we have committed. What I am saying is that many illnesses have their origins in the mind and spirit, and that when we experience forgiveness we begin to experience healing of the whole person. It is also true that many people who experience physical healing, yet remain without Christ, after a time fall ill to the same sickness. Due to this we should not be surprised when people turn to witches or charlatans for healing from illness when they remain sick. Those who turn to Jesus with the same attitude, many times suffer the same result. God is interested, above all, in healing our spirits, and as a result of this, our illnesses. Christ himself said in the sermon on the mount "Be concerned above everything else with the kingdom of God and with what he requires of you, and he will provide you with all these other things". And in James 5:14-16 God says "Is there anyone who is sick? He should send for the church elders, who will pray for him and rub olive oil on him in the name of the Lord. This prayer made in faith will heal the sick person; the Lord will restore him to health, and the sins he has committed will be forgiven. So then, confess your sins to one another and pray for one another, so that you will be healed. The prayer of a good person has a powerful effect." In this story, prayer for healing depends on the confession of our sins. If we want physical, mental or emotional healing, we need to begin from a base of spiritual healing and the rest will come in addition to this.

The four friends of the paralytic went to Jesus in search of physical healing yet Jesus knew what the man really needed, and gave them more than they came for. This is who God is, we ask Him for two things and he gives us four. They met not only a miracle worker, but the Son of God himself, the God of all creation, and as a result of this discovery by faith, four important things resulted:

Healing

When Jesus said to the paralytic "Stand up, take your mat, and go on home, because you are healed", the text tells us that immediately he got up, took his mat and went home. The only thing that Jesus needed to say was "rise", in other words, "be healed." He never prayed for the sick, he directly healed them. Jesus had been anointed by God to heal the broken, and this was one of the first experiences He had in putting into practice this calling.

Worship

The paralytic, after rising to his feet, took his mat and went home glorifying God, as did those who had seen the miracle. When Jesus does a miracle, whether it be physical or spiritual, our reaction needs to be one of worship. However, we need to worship God always, not just in special moments, because He is God and deserves the adoration of His people.

Amazement

The village paralytic got up, took his bed and walked to his house. It was the first time that he did not need his friends. This same amazement happens today when we see people, those we thought would never become Christians, accept Christ as Savior, or when God does miracles in the lives of others. Someone has said that faith is a mental attitude, where we deliberately make room for God to surprise us. One of the principle reasons for our Christian monotony is that we do not make room for God in our minds and hearts so that God can surprise us.

Fear

They were filled with fear because they had seen extraordinary things. What were they? Not only did Jesus make a paralytic walk, but they had discovered that they were face to face with someone who was more than a common, everyday human being. They discovered that they had encountered someone with divine powers, who knew their thoughts and forgave sins.

How do we approach Jesus? Do we approach him with faith or with doubt? If it is with doubt, God will not surprise us. God desires for us to approach Him in faith, whether it be to receive the forgiveness of sins or to receive healing. He is the King of Kings and the Lord of Lords. He is the same yesterday, today and forever. The story is told of a missionary re-union celebrated on the island of Raratanga. An older man rose up and said: "I have lived through the reigns of four kings. During the first we had ongoing warfare, and we all lived in fear. During the reign of the second we suffered from hunger to the point where we ate rats, grass and wood. During the time of the third king we were a beaten and subdued people who suffered invasion. But during the reign of the fourth king we were visited by another king, the Great King, Jesus Christ, the king of love, of power, the king of heaven. He has conquered our hearts and for this reason we have peace, healing, plenty in this world, the hope of living with him in the next.

The question that we must answer is, has Jesus conquered our hearts? The victorious Christian life does not consist of having a monopoly on the Holy Spirit and on His gifts, rather that the Holy Spirit control our hearts, our lives and all that we are and have. In Jesus there are possibilities of an abundant life and a fruitful one. We only need to go to Him in faith, with room in our minds and hearts so that He can surprise us.

Study Guide

Introduction

Briefly relate the story of Joseph Smith, the prophet and founder of the Mormons.

Transitional Phrase

On a certain occasion Jesus said: "Blessed are those who haven't seen me and believe anyway" (John 20:29b) Nevertheless, he did many miracles during his earthly ministry. What we will see in this time together is that these miracles were done to show that He was God.

Bible Reading

Luke 5:17-26; Matthew 9:2-8 and Mark 2:3-12.

In this biblical account we can see three great discoveries that the characters made, and then we will see some of the results.

1. They discovered His power to heal

The same power that Jesus had received the day of his baptism in the Jordan River was with him now to bring about miracles and to teach. Jesus has not changed and desires that we trust in him with whatever our needs are.

2. They discovered His Omnipresence

They not only discovered that Jesus had the power to heal, but that he was also able to know the most intimate thoughts of men. Jesus knows exactly what we think and feel. Nothing escapes him.

3. They discovered his Divinity

The central theme of this account is the divinity of Jesus. The argument is that only God is able to forgive sins and if Jesus did it, therefore He also is God.

4. Results

The results of these discoveries were basically four: healing, worship, amazement and fear.

Conclusion

If we approach Jesus with faith, He will surprise us with some miracle.

Questions for study and discussion

1. Where was Jesus when he healed the paralytic and forgave his sins?

2. What did it mean that Scribes and teachers of the law had come from many far places?

3. The power of the Lord was with Jesus to heal. To what important event does this refer?

4. How is it known that the four were friends, if Luke does not state this?

5. What were the houses like in the time of Jesus?

6. For whose faith was the paralytic healed?

7. What attribute of God did Jesus exhibit upon knowing what the Scribes and Pharisees were thinking?

8. If Jesus was able to forgive sins, what did this imply? Were the Scribes and Pharisees right when thinking that only God was able to forgive sins?

9. What is the relation in this biblical event between healing and forgiveness?

10. What were some of the results of this double miracle?

Applicational Activities

1. Each person has an area of their lives that is paralyzed. In what areas of your life are you hoping that Jesus will intervene?

2. Four friends carried a paralytic to Jesus. What implications does this have for your life?

3. In what way might your faith participate in some miracle in the life of another person? Who are some people that you would like to "carry to Jesus"?

4. What are the doubts, thoughts and questions that you have? Present them to Jesus, in any case, He knows what you think and feel.

5. How do you respond when God intervenes in your life or in the lives of others?

Appetizer for the Soul III

✝

A true christian

A man who had just accepted Christ as savior, ran with all of his strength on the Road of Life, looking all around and searching. He approached an older man who was seated along side the road and asked him "Excuse me, have you see a Christian pass by?" The older man, intimidated de hombre, answered "It depends what type of Christian you are looking for." "I'm sorry," said the man, "but I am new to this and I don't know about the different types of Christians, I only know Jesus." The old man responded "Well, dear friend, there are many types of believers, depending on what one likes. There are Christians of performance, of tradition, of custom, of superstition, of obligation, of convenience, and then there are authentic Christians.

"The authentic Christians! These are the ones I look for! I want the true Christians!" "Then go" said the old man in a grave voice. "These are the most difficult ones to find. It has been a long time since I have seen one pass by here, and he asked me the same question that you did."

"How can I recognize him?" asked the new believer. The old man answered calmly "Don't worry, friend. You will not have a problem recognizing him. A true Christian can not go unnoticed in a world of learned and vain people. You will recognize him for his works. Where a true believer goes, he will always leave footprints4.

Chapter Four

†

Characters of a true story

One day while Jesus was teaching, some Pharisees and teachers of religious law were sitting nearby. (It seemed that these men showed up from every village in all Galilee and Judea, as well as from Jerusalen). And the Lord's healing power was strongly with Jesus. Some men came carring a paralyzed man on a sleeping mat. They tried to push through the crowd to Jesus, but they couldn't reach him. So they went up to the roof, took off some tiles, and lowered the sick man down into the crowd, still on his mat, right in front of Jesus. Seeing their faith, Jesus said to the man, "Son, your sins are forgiven". "Who does this man think he is?" the Pharisees and teachers of religious law said to each other. "This is blasphemy! Who but God can forgive sins?". Jesus knew what they were Thinking, so he asked them, "Why do you think this is Blasphemy?. It is easier to say, 'Your sins are forgiven' or 'Get up and wald'. I will prove that I, the Son of Man, have the authority on earth to forgive sins". Then Jesus turned to the paralyzed man and said, "Stand up, take your mat, and go on home, because you are healed". And inmediately, as everyone watched, the man jumped to his feet, picked up his mat, and went home prising God. Everyone was gripped whit great wonder and awe. And they praised God, saying over and over again, "We have seen amazing things today".

Luke 5:17-26 (See Matthew 9:2-9; and Mark 2:3-12).

It was Friday, the third of May, 1974. In the northeast of Argentina, a young nine year old boy got up that morning to go to school with his brothers and sister, as they did every day. But that morning he could not go as he woke up with a painful headache. The next day his parents took him to a nearby clinic.

Diagnosis: Meningitis.

Probability of Survival: Very small chance

Probability of living a healthy life if he survived: No Chance

Reaction of family: Prayer

After five days of unconsciousness, the young child astounded his doctors and the hospital personnel by rapidly recovering. 14 days later, he returned home, completely healed with no trace or consequence of the deadly illness.

I can relate this story with joy as I was the young child who awoke with the painful headache. How can I not believe in miracles? How can I not believe that Christ can heal us today as he did me when I was young?

In the gospel of Luke, chapter 5: 17-26, we read of a transforming encounter that a man had with Jesus. Even if in chapter 3 I focuse more on Christ's attributes, in this chapter the author wants to get back to other spiritual truths or principles that serve to encourage the reader. Everyone suffers from some type of paralysis and no one is completely sane. Keeping this in mind, we all can approach Jesus with the hope or expectation the he is able to do something in our lives. If we don't create a space in our hearts and minds, if we don't approach Him in expectation or hope, we can't expect to experience his miracles for us. These biblical account is comprised of five different groups of people:

The Pharisees and teachers of the law

These were the students of the Old Testament. Luke says that they came from many places; some had traveled 100 miles or so to be there. These shows us the fame that Jesus had. Why did they come? With a doubt they came to hear what Jesus was teaching as they were considered the guardians of the truth. As such, they considered it their duty to criticize him.

We can fall in the same attitude as that of the scribes and pharisees of yesteryear. We can hope to be teachers, the guardians of the truth, and make it impossible for the Holy Spirit to teach us new and hidden things that God has promised to give those with a searching heart. During the days of the prophet Jeremiah the people of Israel were going through a difficult time. Babylonia was reading to strike and defeat the nation, and would soon take many captive. It is interesting that Jeremiah, in the midst of many messages dealing with God's justice and wrath, also speaks of hope for the people. Jeremiah says "Ask me and I will tell you some re-markable secrets about what is going to happen here" This same promise is also for us today. When we shut ourselves off emotionally, mentally and spiritually to the work of God, we run the risk of becoming Pharisees and scribes, open to defending the "truth" without valuing the need for love and mercy. The spiritual mana that God can give us today, tomorrow will be old, as He will have something new tomorrow for us as well.

The four friends of the paralytic

The Gospel of Mark tells us that there were four. These four play an important role in this story, as the healing of the paralytic depended greatly on them. There are at least four character traits that they had that we can imitate:

Sensitivity to those in need

They realized that the paralytic could have never have got to where Jesus was without help, so they decided to take him themselves. The account does not tell us if the the paralytic or the friends came up with the idea. What we don't know if that these four friends had not taken this walk of faith, the paralytic would have lost the opportunity to receive healing.

Around us there are thousands of people who are spiritually paralyzed. They are hoping that we can talk them to meet Jesus, that we will show them the way to know Jesus. It has been shown that if four people are invited to participate in a church activity, one will accept. This person would not come by himself or herself, as often our natural tendencies don't lend to a personal search for God. It is told that a Christian man lived in a residential community, and every Sunday got ready to go the church. At the same time his neighbor got ready to play golf. At times the golfer had invited his neighbor to play golf with him, yet the Christian always responded that he had to go to church. One day the neighbor asked his church going friend "I have invited you a number of times to play golf, yet you have not invited me to church. Why? " The questions that we must answer is, how many people have we invited to attend a church or other Christian activity?

Perseverance

When the friends of the paralytic saw the multitude surrounding the house with Christ inside, they did not go back home nor did they say "Let's go home and come back another day." They also did not quietly stand in line. They decided to climb to the terrace, make a hole and lower their friend from there.

In that period, houses were made of clay and rock, and the roof made of clay and straw, sustained by wooden supports. They removed the straw and clay and lowered down the paralytic. The problems of how they were going to do this did not hinder them, and their friend was soon next to Jesus.

Our natural tendency is to share Christ with someone just one time and go away thinking that we have done our job. It has been shown that for someone to make a decision for Jesus, he or she has to have heard the gospel, or a part of it, at least 14 times. As such we should not lose our patience, but should persevere. Perseverance is key to help make the projects and dreams of God in our lives and in the lives of others a reality.

Faith

What motivated them to persevere in their faith was the faith that they had in Jesus Himself, upon seeing them, recognized that they were men of great faith. Luke says "Jesus saw their faith" (v 20). Without faith it is impossible to please God; without faith it is impossible to be the beneficiaries of God's blessings, blessings that he has prepared for us. Faith is a mental attitude through which we are able to make a space in our hearts and minds so that God can surprise us with a miracle. It does not matter how many years one has been a Christian, if one doesn't nurture this space he or she can not be a receiver of His blessings. While we cannot make others Christians, our words and acts, brought into being through a spiritual space, can help smooth the way so that others will take the Path of Life.

The Cost of Faith

This aspect is very important. The four friends not only opened them-selves to the jests of others, to criticism, or to the wrath of the house's owner, but were also ready to invest economically, as later they surely paid the owner of the house for the needed repairs. They also paid the price for the insults and ridicule. I suppose that all those who found themselves the recipients of falling clay and straw were not too happy either, even they probably added their insults.

If we as the church are not ready to invest economically in the lost, we cannot expect that God will bless us. I remember a congregation that had a good deal of money in the bank, but spiritually was moribund. Its lead-ership was not willing to invest in those that did not know Christ. We must invest not only money, but also our capacities, gifts, talents and time, not only during an evangelistic campaign, but always.

The Paralytic

The third group is comprised of the paralytic. Even if his role is physically passive, without a doubt he displayed an active faith. He allowed his friends to take him, or possibly he even initiated the story, and ran the risk of not being healed. He obeyed when Jesus told him to rise, take his mat and go home. Once healed, he returned home worshipping God for his blessings.

Each time that we have an encounter with the real Jesus, our hearts display a gratitude towards him for all of his blessings. If later, in a meeting, or upon returning to our work we lose this gratitude, even due to something simple, we did not have a real encounter with Christ. A real encounter with Jesus obliges us to remain thankful. Gratitude is a characteristic of a heart changed for Jesus.

The multitude

The multitude played the role of spectators. At the beginning they ap-peared to be pressing in on Jesus and keeping the four friends and the paralytic from approaching Christ. Later they ended up being admirers and worshipping God for the marvelous things that they had seen.

Today in evangelical churches there are thousands of Christian spectators, who only go to see a show, to see what the church can offer them o to see how God can bless others. They marvel at His works and return to their homes amazed at what the Lord did in the lives of others. These same people never allow Jesus to do this in their lives.

In the Christian life we can be spectators or players. As players we can help others, in the same way that the four friends helped the paralytic, o we can be direct recipients of a blessing by Jesus.

God wants all of his children to be involved, and not remain as spectators who view from a distance what God is doing. Here in Argentina when a soccer team wins a championship, the fans celebrate. Yet it is the players themselves who celebrate most.

Jesus

He is the main character of this story. Luke says that He was teaching and the power of the Lord was manifested through his healing of sick people. This makes reference to Luke 4:18,19 , when Jesus took the promise from the Old Testament by saying:: "The Spirit of the Lord is on me, because he has anointed me to preach good news to the poor. He has sent me to proclaim freedom for the prisoners and recovery of sight for the blind, to release the oppressed, to proclaim the year of the Lord's favor."

The main purpose of this passage, as we have anticipated, is to demonstrate that Jesus is God. When He told the paralytic: "Your sins have been forgiven", the Pharisees and the Scribes began to murmur that He had blasphemed, because only God can forgive sins. And they were right, But as Jesus knew their thoughts He asked them: "Which is easier, to say your sins are forgiven?" which was very difficult to prove, "or to say, 'Get up and walk?'", which everybody could know whether it was true or not.

In order to show the audience that Jesus was God, He healed the paralytic not only physically but also spiritually, and those who criticized Him had nothing more to say. On this episode, Jesus fulfills two messianic characteristics: to forgive sins and heal the sick.

Jesus also wants to bless us. He does not want us to be just listeners to His Word or spectators of His power. He wants us also to be doers of His

Word and protagonists of His power, and to put our faith to work.

God can heal us immediately or progressively, the key is to put our trust and faith in Him constantly, and that we may see Him us Jehova Rophe, like our healer. As Jesus worked a miracle of healing in my own life, thus He is still interested in reaching out his hands towards each one of us and bless us.

Study guide
Introduction

Make a summary of the child's story or tell another story or personal testimony.

Transitional phrase

If Jesus has done this miracle in my life and in the life of others in the past, ¿why wouldn't He do a miracle in our lives today?

Bible reading

Luke 5:17-26, Mathew 9:2-8 and Mark 2:3-12

In this story we find five different groups of people, who reflect our own approach to reality.

1. Pharisees and teachers of the law

They were those who studied the law, but were spiritually hermetic to a new truth. No matter how many years we have as believers, we should always have an open heart so that God may surprise us.

2. The four friends of the sick man

They play an important role in this story, because through them the miracle was made possible by taking the paralytic to Jesus. Basically, we can learn four things through them: sensitivity to those who are in need, perseverance, faith and its cost.

3. The paralytic

Though he played a passive role physically, spiritually his faith was active. His healing brought gratitude and joy. A personal encounter with Jesus makes us more thankful.

4. The crowd

At first, they were just observers, but they ended up praising and glorifying God. The Lord expect us to be protagonists in His kingdom.

5. Jesus

He is the protagonist in the story. His capacity to forgive and to heal shows that He is God.

Conclusion

God does not want us to be listeners to His word, but also makers of His word. He invites us to put our faith in action. No matter what kind of paralysis we might live, Jesus invites us to reach out to Him.

Questions for study and discussion

1. The text says that Jesus was teaching, what was He teaching on?

2. Who were the pharisees and the teachers of the law?

3. Does the fact that the power of the Lord was present in Jesus to heal imply any difference towards the powers of miracles and teaching?

4. Why did they want to put the paralytic in front of Jesus?

5. What would have been the cost of opening a hole on the roof? How would those present have reacted?

6. Why did the scribes and the pharisees think that Jesus spoke blasphemy when He forgave the paralytic's sins?.

7.Whom had Jesus taken authority from?

8. Can a miracle bring faith or is faith carrying out miracles?

9. Can someone be surprised at God's works and even glorify Him, but not be born again?

Applicational activities

1. Which of the groups of people appearing in this story do you feel more identified with? Why?

2. Which are the principles that both the pharisees and the scribes have in their hearts?

3. How many people have you lately taken Jesus' message to?

4. If there is a power in God to heal, is it possible that we may obtain the same?

5. In which sence a miracle has worked out faith in you?

Appetizer for the Soul V

†

A hidden treasure

It was a day like any other. A simple farmer was plowing in his fields.

Hearing a noise under the plow, he discovered that he had unearthed a trunk full of gold coins. Astonished at this immense fortune, he dragged the trunk up to his house and buried it in his garden.

Over the next few days, he thought continuously about what he would do with the treasure. With it he could buy anything, and could go anywhere. Yet, upon further reflection, he decided to leave it hidden. Realizing that the treasure could solve almost any problem he might have, he figured that it would always be there to meet any unforeseen need.

The hidden treasure was so reassuring to the farmer that over time his character changed substantially. He became relaxed and more at ease with himself and with life. Confidence replaced fear, and security took away his anxieties. Life's hardships eased, and he came to believe that life could be a beautiful and happy experience. His hidden treasure had changed him.

His radical life change not only benefited him, but also benefited his family and friends. He became an influential man in his town, thinking of others and their betterment. Over the years his good deeds and hard work made him a regional hero. Many years later, on his deathbed, this once humble plowman gathered his children and finally revealed his incredible and well kept secret. He then died in peace.

Very early the following day, his sons dug up the trunk and eagerly looked inside. Yet to their surprise it was empty. Ten years previous, fortune hunters had stolen the treasure.

The story begs the question. What was the real treasure? It was not the FACT of being rich that gave reassurance to our hero, but the THOUGHT that such riches existed that gave him such a dramatic life change. The story shows the power of one's thought life.

When we are weighed down or overwhelmed by feelings of unhappiness, neglect, unworthiness, and feeling ignored, or when we want retribution for a wrong done to us, we should consider if our thought patterns are being influenced too much by the world around us. Perhaps it might be better to change the course of these thoughts and unbury our spiritual treasure5. In Jesus Christ, God paid the price so that each one of us can experience a transforming life change, and in this way we may impact others.

Chapter Five

†

The utmost need

Later, as Jesus left the town, he saw a tax collector
named Levi sitting at his tax-collection booth. «Come, be my
disciple!» Jesus said to him. So Levi got up, left everything,
and followed him. Soon Levi held a banquet in his home
with Jesus as the guest of honor. Many of Levi's fellow
tax collectors and other guests were there. But the Pharisees
and their teachers of religion law complained bitterly to
Jesus' disciples, «Why do you eat and drink with such
scum?» Jesus answered them, «Healthy people don't
need a doctor - sick people do. I have come to call sinners
to turn from their sins, not to spend my time with
those who think they are already good enough.»

Luke 5:27-32 (See also Matthew 9:9-13 and Mark 2:14-22)

In Scripture, Jesus narrated the parable of the wedding banquet. He said that a man prepared a great feast and invited the «cream of the crop». As the dinner was being readied, he sent his servant to tell the guests: «Come because everything is ready.» Yet rather than accepting the invitation, the guests sent back «excuses». One said «I bought a piece of land and I must go and see it; please, forgive me.» Another man said: «I bought five yokes of oxen and I am going to try them out; please, forgive me.» Yet another said: «I've just gotten married and can't make it, forgive me.»

When the servant came back and informed his master what had happened, the latter, enraged, said, «Go to the streets and bring me the poor, the lame, the blind and the crippled.» The servant did this, only to find that there was still room at the table. Seeing this, the master sent him into other lesser-reached places in order to fill his banquet hall. When all of this was done, the master forbade the original guests to even participate in his banquet.

Jesus has often chosen the weak and despicable of the world to shame the acknowledged and the self-sufficient. This parable teaches us that many who are apparently invited will not participate in the wedding of the Lamb, and it also teaches us that many Christians who had the possibility to enjoy God's spiritual treats will have to content themselves with bread crumbs, as a consequence of the hardness of their hearts or their indifference.

The following story from the Gospel of Luke deals with a man of high society who was transformed by Jesus. One of the story's basic lessons is that only those who admit their need for God will find His help.

Mathew

This is the story of the calling of Mathew the tax collector. Out of all the people in Palestine, the tax collectors were the most lonely and hated. We might think of Zacheus, for example, one of the many outcasts of Israelite society. By Jesus' time, the great Israelite empire had dwindled down tosimply the occupation of Palestine, as the Jews were now dominated by theRoman Empire. Some Jews, working for the empire as tax collectors, would collect taxes from their fellow Jews, often keeping a portion for themselves. They were seen as unworthy traitors, or renegades, who sold out their fellow Jews for money.

William Barclay has written that the tax system was prone to abuses. The Roman custom consisted in paying a commission for tax collecting; thus, in a way, the tax system was private. The Romans settled an area and basically outsourced it for tax purposes. A tax collector had to collect a certain amount of taxes for the empire, what was left over he could keep for himself. As it was a society without mass communications, people often did not know how much they should pay, and were at the mercy of the tax collectors and an overwhelming tax system.

First, there was an enrollment tax that every man between fourteen and seventy five years and every woman between twelve and seventy five paid for the simple privilege of being alive. There was also a tax on the land, which consisted of paying 10% of the harvest and 20% of wine and oil. There was also an income tax of 1%. Due to the structure of the system, there were many, many opportunities to overcharge.

Second, there were taxes on almost everything: for using main roads, ports and markets, there were fees for carts, and for every wheel and for every animal used to pull it. There were taxes on trade and for imports and exports. A tax collector was able to stop someone in route, make him unpack his cart and charge him an amount the tax collector considered to be «fair». If the person was unable to pay, the tax collector might loan him the money at an exorbitant rate, putting the traveler even more in debt. It is small wonder that someone like Zacheus or Matthew was so odious to his countrymen!

Tax collectors or publicans were regarded as thieves and assassins. They were not allowed to go into the synagogue. A roman writer gives an account on having seen a monument to an honest tax collector. This shows how difficult it was to find an honest one. For some people it would be like trying to find an honest politician or lawyer!6

Tax collectors were rejected by almost everybody. To the scribes and Pharisees they were the worst of sinners. Mathew belonged to that group; and he was hated and rejected by his people. Nevertheless, it is him who Jesus calls to be one of His disciples. In this story we find three different groups of people.

Mathew, who realized that Jesus accepted him the way he was, accepted the invitation to follow Him and turned to Christ. First, he invited Jesus to a party. He was able to do so, for he had enough money. He invited his friends and partners, those neglected by society, to meet Jesus. Mathew's first reaction was to share his wonderful experience, which he could not keep to himself. As I write, I question how willingly we might go to a party that someone is giving on stolen money. It might be easier for us to apply the law instead of His grace!

Mathew's attitude shows us that if our experience with Jesus is genuine we will not be able to keep it to ourselves. We may tend to have dinner with brothers and sisters in our church very frequently rather than with people who don't know Jesus. John Wesley, founder of the Methodist Church, said «no man goes to heaven alone, he must find some friends or make them.»7 In the story, we observe a principle of discipleship from the beginning of conversion: Mathew became Jesus' disciple and «straightway» began to share the gospel and make disciples automatically.

Jesus

Jesus did not only invite Mathew to follow Him, but He also sat at a table with men and women who were outcasts like Mathew, notable among them were publicans, prostitutes and other sinners. It is as if Jesus was intrinsically repeating the banquet parable, as if He was saying «When you give a party you invite the most orthodox there are; those who take pride in virtue, those who think of themselves as good. But I share my time and my resources with those who are more aware of their sins and their need of God.» This was quite shocking to the Pharisees and Scribes, but acceptable for sinners. Jesus' attitude is the psychological healing that every outcast needs. First, they need to be accepted just as they are and then they need to be helped to change.

In general, Palestine was divided in two categories: the orthodox who observed the law to the minutest detail and the common people who did not pay much attention to its strict stipulations. The orthodox were forbidden to travel with them, trade with them, to give or receive something from them, or to have them as guests or to go to their houses. By joining these people, Jesus was doing something that no religious orthodox would have dared to do.

Jesus had a simple reason for behaving this way. He simply went to places where there was greater need. It would not be a good physician who visited only healthy people; the place for a physician is with the sick. Diogenes, one of the greatest philosophers of Ancient Greece, never ceased to compare the decadent life in Athens, where he lived most of his life, to the simplicity and strictness of Sparta. One day, somebody who was tired of the comparisons told him: «If you think that Sparta is so wonderful and Athens is so despicable why don't you leave Athens and go to Sparta?» The philosopher's answer was «It doesn't matter what I might prefer, my duty is to remain where men most need me.» Those who most needed Jesus were the sinners, and Jesus lived his life among them. In the same way, sinners are those who most need to be invited to come to Jesus, not those who think of themselves as good.

Times have not changed and those having spiritual, psychological, physical and or emotional sickness are those who find Jesus most quickly. When Jesus said: «I did not come to invite the righteous but to invite the sinners» He did not mean that the good and healthy needed nothing from Him. What He meant was, basically «I have not come to invite people so pleased with themselves and who are so sure of their goodness or those who believe that they do not need anybody's help. I have come to invite those who are aware of their sins and who know they desperately need a Savior. Only those who know to what extent they need me are able to accept my invitation.» Once Epictetus called Jesus teachings «the medicine of salvation»8.

According to Jesus, only the sick need a physician and people like Mathew and his friends were who most needed Him. Nowadays, we should regard sinners as sick and needy instead of criminals and we should regard those who make mistakes not as misfits and condemned but as people who need love and help to find the right way.

Scribes and Pharisees

This group did not agree with Jesus. They could not even allow part of their tunic to touch a man like Mathew. Nevertheless, Jesus gave them the right answer. There are many orthodox Christians in churches who have little regard for those who come from a lower economic or social level. Recently, I read a notice that said, «Poor relatives are distant relatives.»

Unfortunately, many Christians act on this premise more often than not and we treat people as the scribes and Pharisees treated publicans and sinners. This is why James warned the primitive church that every human being deserves the right to be treated as an equal, as beings created to God's image. Yet the scribes and Pharisees interpreted religion in the same way that many people do nowadays. I remember that in one of the churches that my wife and I pastored, the first people who came to join our congregation, which for many years had been decreasing, were the socially secluded and depressed. At one prayer meeting, a believer of higher socioeconomic standing expressed his concern at having the church full of sick and crazy people.» In Jesus' time, Pharisees and scribes were also worried what these people were entering God's Kingdom. One might describe the scribes and Pharisees as sharing four characteristics:

a) They were more worried at preserving their own sanctity than in helping others overcome their sins. They were like physicians who do not want to assist AIDS patients for fear of getting the disease. They were repelled by sinners and did not want to have anything to do with them. Their religion was essentially selfish and they went astray rather than helping the needy.

b) They were more concerned about criticizing wrongs than developing holiness in others. They were more ready to condemn everybody else's mistakes than to lead others to spiritual victory. Our first instinct should never be to condemn sinners, but to look for a way to help them.

c) They practiced a particular form of «kindness» that resulted in condemnation rather than forgiveness or sympathy. They helped their own, but would leave a sinner in the ditch rather than stretch out their hands to help him. They were like physicians capable of diagnosing illnesses but having no intention of curing them. They were busy looking down on others, rather than building them up.

d) They practiced a religion consisting of exterior orthodoxy rather than initiating positive principles for a practical present. Jesus had great esteem for Hosea 6:6 as he cited it repeatedly: «I desire mercy, not sacrifice.» The religious man can carry out every ritual: praying, Bible reading, congregating, giving offerings, paying tithes, but if he has never stretched out his hand to help the sinner nor the one in need, his is not the Christian that Christ desires him to be.

We can draw three main points from this story. First, we observe that Jesus came for those who recognize their need of Him. They may be black or white, well-educated or ignorant, man or woman, elderly or children, rich or poor; anyone who recognizes his need for Jesus can go to Him.

Second, our attitude towards the needy must be the same as Jesus and not like one of the scribes or Pharisees. He came to look for and save what was lost. We have to put off our legalism and allow Jesus to cover our hearts with a great cloak of grace.

Third, as He did to Mathew, Jesus invites you to follow Him, to give a party and invite your non-Christian friends or relatives to share what Jesus has done in your life. He expects a positive response from you. If you are aware of your need of God, you can go confidently to Jesus and find a place in His arms. If you rest in Jesus, you can also experience the joy of a feast like Mathew's, as he knew he was accepted and forgiven by Jesus.

Study guide
Introduction

Write a brief summary of the parable of the great banquet (Luke 14:15-24 or Matthew 22:1-10) emphasizing how those who were first invited to the party did not participate in the banquet.

Transition phrase

Mathew's story is a story in which the person invited responded immediately to Jesus' invitation. Mathew is presented as a man in need.

Bible reading

Luke 5:27-32, Matthew 9:9 -13 and Mark 2:14-22.

In this narration we encounter the calling of Matthew. Although Matthew is the main character, yet there are other stories to note as well.

1. Mathew

Tax collectors were considered as betrayers to their nation; thus, they were marginalized both by society and the religious system-which saw them as robbers and sinners. Yet the tax collector Mathew recognized himself as being in need, accepted Jesus' invitation and gave a party in which he invited his friends and partners. Like Matthew, Jesus expects us to share His Word with those who are really in need.

2. Jesus

Jesus not only invited Mathew to follow Him, but to also sit at His table.

Jesus' strategy was simple: He just went where there was the greater need.

Times have changed, but the needy are still here and it is to them to whom we should take the good news.

3. Scribes and Pharisees

They did not agree with Jesus. They are defined by four characteristics:

a. They were most worried about themselves.

b. They were more involved in criticizing others than in building them up.

c. They cultivated a «kindness» based on condemnation and not on grace.

d. They practiced a religion based more on exterior practice than on character development.

Conclusion

Jesus has come to save us all and we can go to and learn from Him. As in the case of Mathew, Jesus invites us and wants a positive response to His call.

Questions for study and discussion

1. The text begins by saying «After that...» Which is the event that precedes this miracle?

2. Who were the tax collectors?

3. What showed that Jesus was interested in Mathew?

4. Would Mathew have previously heard of Jesus? What would he have seen in

Jesus so as to leave it all and follow Him?

5. Why would Mathew have given a party for Jesus at his place?

6. What would have motivated Mathew to invite other tax collectors to his party?

7. Why did scribes and Pharisees complain about Jesus going to the party? What was their view of tax collectors?

8. In the time of Jesus, hat did it imply to share a table with sinners?

9. What did Jesus think about Scribes and Pharisees and what did He think about publicans?

10. What are the reasons Jesus spent time with outcasts?

Application activities

1. What are those things in your life that tend to separate you from others? Is this by your own initiative?

2. What does it personally mean to you that Jesus was interested in Mathew?

3. Have you ever given a party for Jesus where you invited others to know what has happened spiritually in your life?

4. What does it means to you when Jesus says that He did not come to look for the healthy but for the sick?

5. What is your attitude towards those marginalized by society? How could that attitude change or improve?

Appetizer for the Soul VI

†

Puzzle

A scientist, worried about the world's ills and determined to find the means to alleviate them, spent his days in his lab looking for an answer to his quests. One day, his 7-year-old son came in determined to help him in his work. The scientist, bothered by the interruption, asked the child to go to play somewhere else. Finding it impossible to get him to leave, the father looked for something to keep him busy. Finding a magazine that contained a good size world map, he cut the map into small bits with a pair of scissors and he gave it to the boy with some scotch tape saying: «Since I know you like puzzles, I made one for you. Try and put the world back together all by yourself.»

The scientist thought that it would take days for the boy to put the map back together, but it was not the case. A few hours later, he heard the child's voice calling him softly. «Daddy, I did it! I finished it.» At first, the father paid no attention to the child's words. He thought it impossible for a child his age to put a map back together so quickly, especially one that he had never seen before. Distrustful, he glanced away from his work, expecting to find a world map incorrectly pieced together. To his surprise, the map was complete. All the pieces had been put in the right place. How was it possible? How had his son been able to do it?

The father asked, «Son, you did not know what the world is like. How did you manage to piece it back together so well and so quickly?

His son replied, «Dad, I did not know what the world was like, but when you took out the map from the magazine to cut it, I saw that on the other side there was a man. So I just turned the pieces over and started to put together the man. When I finished putting the man together, I turned the page and saw that I had fixed the world.

«If I changed, the world would change.»9 When God changes our lives, there will be possibilities for us to be used to change the world. A transforming encounter with Jesus can make a world of difference.

Chapter Six

†

Paralysis vs. Movement

On another Sabbath day, a man with a deformed right
hand was in the synagogue while Jesus was teaching.
The teachers of religious law and the Pharisees watched
closely to see whether Jesus would heal the man on Sabbath,
because they where eager to find some legal charge to
bring against him. But Jesus knew their thoughts. He said
to the man with the deformed hand, «Come and stand
where here everyone can see». So the man came forward.
Then Jesus said to his critics, «I have a question for
You. Is it legal to do good deeds on the Sabbath, or
Is it a day for doing harm? Is this a day to save life or to
Destroy it?». He looked around at them one by one
And then said to the man, «Reach out your hand.»
The man reached out his hand, and it became
Normal again!. At this, the enemies of Jesus
were wild with rage and began to discuss
what to do with him.

Luke 6:6-11 (See also Matthew 12:9 -14 and Mark 3:1-6).

Once there was a ship wreck near an uninhabited island. Its one survivor swam to shore, carrying with him some things of the ship. There he built a hut and each day prayed to God that a boat would pass by to rescue him.

One day, his hut caught fire and all he had was destroyed. He thought that it was the worst thing that could have happened to him, but a few hours later a ship came and the captain told him «As soon as we saw the smoke signal you sent, we came.»

A calamity can shake a nation, a community or a person, but sometimes it just might be a blessing. The recent terrorist attacks against the United States, the economic, social and political crisis that Argentina is currently going through together with other Latin American countries could be calamities that in some way might awaken a spiritual thirst in many darkened hearts or frightened minds. In general, pain makes us think over the essentials in our lives. It brings to light those things on which we build our life and hope.

This passage in Luke allows us to see from another perspective the way in which calamity or sickness brought the man with a shriveled hand to a transforming encounter with Jesus. It is an experience that can transform us, too.

In the narrative we find three different types of people. First, there was Jesus, who, regardless of religious rules, decided to do what was right and preached at the synagogue. Second, there was the man with a shriveled hand, and third, there were the scribes and Pharisees.

Nowadays, we also find these three types in our churches. There are those who teach, work and serve the Lord; there are those who are spiritually growing and have spiritual needs needing and being met, and there are those who simply observe, judge and criticize, thinking that they know all there is to know about the Christian life.

As odd as it might seem, the latter group hated a man that had cured someone in pain. They are the example of those who love their system more than God himself. Their rules are more precious than God. We observe that this happens sometimes at church. We discuss more about church government and politics rather than about important themes of faith.

A preacher once said, «A church's form of government should be built upon the fruit of the Spirit.» There is always the danger to put one's faithfulness first to a system rather that to God. These scribes and Pharisees were full of hatred and they were thinking of what to do to Jesus rather than rejoicing in a miracle.

When God does something there are always people wondering whether it was Him or not, wondering whether it could have been done another way.

Nevertheless, Jesus shows us in this passage that neither accepted rules nor the opinions of others do not need to govern us when we want to do something good for somebody. In this chapter, we will focus our attention on the man with the shriveled hand. His plight shows us four things applicable to today.

He was a man in need

Nowadays, we live in an individualistic and lonely society. Many people have deep spiritual, physical, and emotional needs. As a consequence of their pride, they do not admit or reveal these needs and present themselves before church and society as self-sufficient, as if they knew everything and as if they did not need anybody or anything.

Yet in this story we find a man, obviously a Jew as he was in a synagogue, who had no problem admitting or revealing his need. He was a man who wanted to know more about the Kingdom of Heaven and, moreover, he had a physical need: a paralyzed hand. This is an interesting point. If we compare this passage to Mathew 12:9-14 and Mark 3:1-6 we notice that only Luke says that the man's right hand was shriveled. As a physician, Luke he was interested in case history details. Evidently, the disabled man needed his hand for work and God honored the man's faith.

Jesus said «Blessed are the poor in spirit, for theirs is the kingdom of heaven. Blessed are those who hunger and thirst for righteousness» (that is, those who admit their need), «for they will be filled.»

He was invited

As Jesus knows people's hearts, undoubtedly he knew the attitude of this man, who surely was not only sick, but also probably ready to admit his need. Jesus had him stand up in front of everyone.

Nowadays, we hear many voices telling us by the media to come here or go there for help, and there are religions that offer temporary help. But among the confusing voices of our modern tower of Babel, there still sounds the eternal echo of the voice of the Great Physician, the voice of the eternal Son of God telling us to rise and go to Him. We still hear Jesus' eternal call: «Come to me, all you who are weary and burdened, and I will give you rest.»

God invites us to still the hollow sounds of others and to tune in to his divine call. We hear God's voice softly saying to us: «I wish to help you, I do not want you to go on suffering, to be in pain, to live wounded, depressed or lonely. Come to me for I want to help you.»

The man with a shriveled hand was paying attention to Jesus' message and suddenly Jesus looked at him and said «Get up and stand in front of everyone». Likewise, He invites us to come to Him with our burdens and difficulties. He wants to give us rest. The world and its ways burdens us with many worries, both economic and social, and prevents us from seeing the stars of God's blessings. We need to stand when Jesus tells us to so that He can surprise us with a miracle.

He was a man who responded to the invitation

What will we do with this eternal invitation by Jesus? If we have stilled all other voices and are tuned in His divine frequency, if we are able hear the sweet and firm invitation of Jesus, let us stand up and go to Him. Possibly, we might need to put this book aside and go to Jesus right now, or perhaps we should do so when this chapter or when this book is finished. When the Spirit calls, we need to answer.

The man with the shriveled hand might have been mocked or laughed at, but he did not care. He was hearing an invitation and tuned out the opinions of others. He walked through the crowd and went to Jesus.

It does not matter the circumstances in our lives. It does not matter if we approach God with a paralyzed hand or heart. As with the man in the biblical narrative, God invites us to put our faith to work and let his miracle happen.

You might think to yourself, «If God wants to help me or bless me, He can do where I am.» Yet we must not put obstacles or conditions on God; we must yield to His ways and we will see His glory. Just as that man had to rise, go to Jesus and extend his hand, God wants us to put our faith in action and He will respond.

God wants to turn our dryness into springs of living water and give us eternal life. He wants to satisfy our thirst and our hunger, and overflow our lives with abundance. Let us not turn deaf ears to his eternal and sweet invitation. Just as the man extended his shriveled hand to Jesus, God wants us to submit our problems to Him and He will do the rest.

He was a man who experienced the results of faith

This man went back home with, undoubtedly, both his hand and his heart healed. He had obeyed God, extended his hand to Jesus, and by this act of faith God healed him.

God wants to fulfill the desires of our hearts. Lets us delight in Him; let us extend now what is paralyzed in our lives so that He can perform his wondrous miracle power.

There is a story on a crippled Indian woman who walked with crutches due to a spine infection. One day she fell down the stairs. She found herself on the floor with one broken crutch at her side and the other one out of her reach. She called for help but nobody heard her.

At last, losing all hope of being heard, with all her faith she prayed to God for strength. Lifting herself on the banister, she stood up and began to walk without crutches.

The best that could have happened to her was that fall, though at the moment it seemed a calamity. But from on high there was a voice saying «Get up and walk.»

It does not matter what our problem might be, God invites us to go to Him and present it to Him. Undoubtedly, it is his will that will be done. Let us now get up and go to Jesus. He will give hope in a world of hopelessness.

Study guide
Introduction

Briefly relate the story of the shipwreck and how the calamity brought rescue to the survivor.

Transition phrase

Calamity may fall upon a person, family or nation, but in light of the Scriptures, we see that it can be a blessing.

Bible reading

Luke 6:6-11; Mathew 12:9-14 and Mark 3:1-6

The man's illness brought him to a transforming encounter with Jesus. The story consists of three main characters: the man with the shriveled hand, the scribes and Pharisees, and Jesus. Our focus will be the man in need.

1. A man in need

He was a Jew, obviously pious, otherwise he would not have been at the synagogue. Yet he was a man with a hand in need. In our society there are many persons in need, though their needs might not be as visible as those of the man in the story.

2. He was invited

As Jesus knew the hearts of people, he saw the man's openness and invited him to come near. Among the many voices that we hear today is the voice of Jesus, calling us to do the same.

3. He responded to the invitation

What shall we do with this eternal invitation? The man in the story shows us a good response; he arose and went forward.

4. He experienced the results of faith

He went back home with his hand healed. His faith in Jesus was not disappointed.

Conclusion

Tell briefly the story of the disabled Indian lady. The problems in our lives are God's best opportunities to glorify himself in us. We should not lose heart; let us trust Him and respond to His invitation. He will never disappoint us.

Questions for study and discussion

1. In which synagogue was Jesus teaching?

2. Why does Luke emphasize the fact that the right hand was the shriveled one?

3. Why were scribes and Pharisees observing Jesus carefully?

4. Which of Jesus' attributes reveals the fact that He knew the thoughts of others?

5. Why did Jesus focus on the sick man in front of others when He could have healed him in private?

6. What is Jesus demonstrating by the question in verse 9? What were His priorities?

7. How do you imagine Jesus looked to those who were present?

8. What was implied when Jesus told the man to stretch out his hand? Could he have done it if it would have still been shriveled?

9. What was the result of this act of faith?

10. Which was the reaction of the scribes and Pharisees before due to the miracle?

Application Activities

1. What are the implications of the fact that out of many people present Jesus had chosen this physically challenged person?

2. Which areas of your life are «shriveled» and need to be renewed or healed by Jesus?

3. In what situations have you acted like the scribes and the Pharisees, putting law before mercy?

4. Which specific changes has Jesus made in your life?

Appetizer for the Soul VII

†

White roses

I went into a downtown shop for some last minute Christmas shopping. I looked at all the people doing what I wanted to quickly get done and began to grumble to myself. I would be there forever, and I had so much to do! Christmas was turning into a headache. I wished I could just hibernate until it was over. I went through the crowd as quickly as I could to the toy section. Once there, I grumbled again over the prices and wondered if my grandchildren would appreciate or play with what they found under the tree on Christmas morning.

Once there, I noticed a boy out of the corner of my eye. He was about five years old and he was hugging a beautiful doll. He stroked her head and held her so tenderly that I continued watching him, wondering whom the doll would be for. He was looking at a woman, his aunt. He called her by her name and asked her «Are you sure we don't have enough money?» The woman answered sadly «You know we don't have enough money to buy that doll.» Then she told the boy not to stay there, as she would return in a few minutes, and left to make some more purchases.

The boy was still hugging the doll, so after a short while I asked him who it was for. He answered, «She's the doll my little sister wanted for Christmas. She was sure she would have it this Christmas.» I told him that maybe his father would give it to her and he told me «No, my father can't go where my sister is. I must give this doll to my mother so that she can take it to her.»

I asked him where his little sister was. He looked at me with sad eyes and said, «She went to be with Jesus. Dad says Mom must go and stay with her.» My heart almost missed a beat. The boy looked at me again and said «I told Dad to ask mom not to go yet, to wait till I got back from the store». Then he asked me if I wanted to see a photo. I said I would love to.

He took out some pictures that had been taken in front of the store and told me «I want Mom to take these pictures with her so that she'll never forget me. I love her so much and I wish she shouldn't leave me, but Dad says she needs to be with my little sister»

I watched the boy put down his head and was silent. While he was not watching, I put my hand in my pocket and took out some money. I asked the boy if he would like it so he could buy the doll. He nodded happily and said he knew it would be enough for the doll. He then said in a soft voice «Thank you Jesus, for giving me the money.» Then he told me» I asked Jesus to give me enough money to buy that doll, so that Mom could take it to my little sister. He heard my prayer. I also wanted to ask Him for money to buy a white rose for Mom, but I didn't. Yet He gave me enough money to buy the doll and the rose for Mom. She loves white roses.»

At that moment, his aunt came back and I left with my cart. I could not stop thinking about the boy as I finished my shopping. I had a completely different attitude than the one I had when I began. I remembered something I had read in the paper some days ago about a drunk driver who had crashed into another car, killing a girl and leaving the mother in serious condition. Their family was deciding if they should unhook the mother from the artificial respiration machine. Yet this little boy certainly could not have been part of this tragic story. Two days later I read that the family had decided to disconnect the mother so that she could die. That same day I went to purchase white roses and took them to the funeral. In the coffin I saw a young lady with a white rose in her hands, the beautiful doll and a picture of the little boy I had seen at the store. I left crying, and my life has never been the same. The love that this little boy had for his mother and sister greatly impacted me10. I encourage you to take a moment and think about a life that you might touch today. We never know what will happen in life, but we can make use of the time we have to make a difference.

Chapter Seven

†

From the heights to the depths

When Jesus had finished saying all this, he went back
to Capernaum. Now he highly valued slave of a Roman
officer was sick and near death. When the officer heard
about Jesus, he sent some respected Jewish leaders to ask
him to come and heal his slave. So they earnestly begged
Jesus to come with them and help the man. «If anyone
deserves your help, it is he», they said, «for he loves the
Jews and even built a synagogue for us». So Jesus went
with them. But just before they arrived at the house, the
officer sent some friends to say, «Lord, don't trouble
yourself by coming to my home, for I am not worthy
of such an honor. I am not even worthy to come and
meet you. Just say the word from where you are,
and my servant will be healed. I know because I am
under the authority of my superior officers, and I have
authority over my soldiers. I only need to say, 'go', and
they go, or 'Come', and they come. Ad if I say to my
slaves, 'Do this or that,' they do it. When Jesus heard
this, he was amazed. Turning to the crowd, he said,
«I tell you, I haven't seen faith like this in all the land
of Israel». And when the officer's friends returned to
his house, they found the slave completely healed.

Luke 7:1-10 (See also Matthew 8:5-13).

Once there was a woman whose husband was soldier in the Union army during the Civil War. She was left alone with four small children to raise, hoping one day to see her husband again.

Among her children, her six-year-old son had learned to trust God, and he was an encouragement to his mother, often bringing joy and hope with his innocent sayings. When the flour jar was almost empty, the mother's worries would be stilled when the small boy observed that it was always filled again as there were many farmers in the area who provided them with what they needed.

One day, while his mother was taking out flour of the jar, the boy was thinking. All of a sudden, an idea crossed his mind. Lifting up his head, he exclaimed «Mom, I think God hears us when we scratch the bottom of the jar!»

Luke's story of the centurion who asked Jesus to heal one of his servants is like the story of the mother who trusted in God. Like the family, God was there for him, too.

Capernaum was a city near the Sea of Galilee in the north of Israel, and it played an important part in the earthly ministry of Jesus. In biblical times, Israel was under the Roman Empire and in each big city there was a centurion, a Roman officer who was in charge of 100 soldiers. In a way, he was the highest authority in the city, as he was the military representative of the empire.

The Jew's main temple was in Jerusalem, and it was the only place where they could offer sacrifices to God; but in each city where there were devout Jews, there was a synagogue or a small temple where they met to study the Scriptures and to engage in other social and teaching activities.

This passage relates the story of the healing of a person who did not meet Jesus, through a person who did not know Jesus. Thus the passage applies to us today, for we often think that seeing is believing. But I want us to focus our attention not on the healed person but on the Roman centurion, from whom we can learn five important things:

He loved his servant

In the Bible we see examples of Roman centurions who had a good attitude towards Christ and His followers. This story shows this clearly.

The narrative says that the centurion loved his servant, a fact which was not very frequent among people from different ranks. We do not know why he loved him, but might conjecture that in part it was because the servant was efficient and reliable. His love was demonstrated though his care, for he was looking for a way to make the servant better. Nowadays in our global world it might be hard to find managers who are as interested in their workers as they are in the bottom line. Unfortunately, this attitude is not only found in secular institutions, but also in Christian ones where God's servants find themselves undervalued. Leaders don't take enough time to talk to them, to know what they think or feel, how they are, to learn about their families, etc. It is well known that one of a person's utmost needs is that of being appreciated, that his job or contribution, no matter how insignificant, be given some kind of recognition. Some shown appreciation could be the remedy for so many people who have been wounded by a pragmatic mentality oriented to productivity. We need to learn from the centurion, who cared enough to send for the very best.

Turning to Jesus

The centurion's care was shown not just in words, but also in deeds. He was so fond of his servant that he cared for him in a practical way, thus going outside of his own religious codes and social class etiquette. When he heard that Jesus was nearby, he decided, through some Jewish elders, to ask Christ to come and heal his servant. We see here character in action. This high-ranking official took the time to care.

Unfortunately, many pastors today remain uncared for. In many institutions and denominations leaders are oriented towards programs rather than towards individuals. Thus, many pastors serve the Lord from hurting lives. Sometimes, the only letter they receive is a notice of an unpaid bill, or the only phone calls they get are impersonal ones. Therefore, many pastors under these circumstances do not know how to pastor their congregations well, as they feel abandoned and marginalized by their own institutional or denominational leaders.

The centurion valued his servant and thus beseeched the help of the Jewish elders. They were not elders due to age but rather due to their position of authority and responsibility within the Jewish community. They went to Jesus and tried to persuade Him by saying that He should help the centurion because the centurion was a good man, that he loved the people of Israel and had built the synagogue. That is, the elders thought that through the centurion's good actions, he deserved Christ's help. Yet Jesus saw in this man more than good works.

Humble in Spirit

We notice that the centurion had a different view of himself. When he saw Jesus approaching he sent some friends to meet him, in order to give the Lord a different perspective. Through these friends, he told Jesus that he was neither worthy of meeting Him nor receiving Him in his house. When we tell God that we have nothing to offer and that we depend on His mercy, only in that moment can God begin to work His miracle in us. Jesus said «Blessed are the poor in spirit, because theirs is the kingdom of heaven.» Pride and arrogance are toxic to the Holy Spirit. It is impossible for God to fill us with His Spirit when He finds us filled with our own ego. First, we need to empty ourselves so that He may fill us with His Spirit. God does not share His glory with anyone: He does it all or He does not do it. One of the most difficult things for us to learn to do is to depend upon His grace.

Spiritual growth includes the important aspect of learning to die to ourselves, to be crucified.

He recognized Jesus' authority

The centurion was able to have the correct attitude towards Jesus because he recognized Jesus' authority as God, something that the Jews did not see. The centurion knew that Jesus was not just another prophet or magician, but that He was God and He was under His Father's authority. He believed that if Jesus said a word, that if He declared his servant healed, he would be healed.

As a result of this active faith in Jesus, the servant was healed and Jesus praised the faith of the centurion by saying that not even in His own nation had he found so much faith. The centurion understood who he was and who Jesus was and recognized the difference.

Nowadays, many come to a Jesus whom they believe to be a miracle worker, a magician, or the owner of a great supermarket who is ready to fill the carts of the saints. Truly Jesus can heal us, restore us, bless us, etc., but He is most interested in finding worshippers who submit willingly to His divinity.

The same Jesus who saved the servant wants to save us. He wants to save you, especially. He wants you to approach him and He will hear you. As the boy said «God hears us better when we scratch the bottom than when we are full». If you love your life, if you love yourself, I urge you to go to God and He will listen.

No matter your social, cultural, or economic conditions, Jesus is there. It doesn't matter what people might say. I urge you to turn to Jesus with the attitude of the centurion. Tell Jesus that you have nothing to offer, that you are unworthy of receiving anything from Him, but that you need His help, His mercy.

The Bible tells us that the wages of our sins is death, which means that each one of us deserves hell. But God did not create us to spend eternity there; He wants us to be with Him forever. Yet though He loves us, He cannot merely excuse our sin.

As none of us can do anything to attain salvation, God took the initiative to solve our problem. The Bible tells us that on the cross Jesus took our sins and paid the debt we had with God; by His wounds we are healed and through His pain we can have peace.

But it is not enough to simply know this fact. The centurion knew Jesus could help him and he turned to Him. You must put your faith in action, you must trust in the work of Jesus Christ on the cross. Saving faith comes when you trust in what Jesus did for you. The centurion, without meeting Jesus, believed in Him and his servant was healed.

The faith that believes without seeing is the faith that God wants for us now. If you recognize that, as in the case of the flour jar, you are scratching the bottom, I invite you to receive Jesus in your heart as your Lord and Savior and the miracle of salvation will take place in your life.

If you wish to experience God's forgiveness for your sins and have the gift of eternal life, don't wait to do so. Whatever your need, go to Jesus; His resources never end. He is always ready to abundantly meet our faith.

Isaiah chapter 55 tells us that Jesus offers us an abundant banquet.

Don't be satisfied with crumbs when we have a banquet awaiting us. After each valley of shadow and death, there are green pastures and a table prepared for us to enjoy a delicious and abundant meal. It is just a question of believing and putting our faith in action. As the old song says:

«Put our faith in action and the miracle will happen.» The centurion did so and his faith was not disappointed.

Study guide
Introduction

Summarize the story of the poor family and how the small boy was able to see that God was helping them in their times of need.

Transitional phrase

Often, when it seems things can't get worse, God provides a way when there seems to be no way.

Bible reading

Luke 7:1-10 and Mathew 8:5-13

This passage narrates the healing of person who did not see Jesus and who was helped by means of another person, the centurion, who did not know Jesus. The centurion's example shows us four character qualities.

1. He was fond of his servant

The text tells us that the centurion was fond of his servant and wanted to do something for him. Our love for people must be obvious and manifested.

Love and appreciation are basic human needs.

2. He turned to Jesus

Appreciation was not only shown by words, but also by action. The centurion was ready to put his reputation at risk for his servant. There are many people around us who are waiting for us to lead them to Jesus, to impact their lives.

3. He was humble in spirit

Some thought Jesus should help the centurion because he was worthy; nevertheless, the centurion did not consider himself as someone who deserved a visit from the Lord. When we scratch the bottom of the jar, when we depend only on God's grace, He meets our need.

4. He recognized Jesus' authority

The centurion was able to come to Jesus in the right way because he previously recognized His authority. Many Christians come to Jesus looking for His blessings, but they do not want to submit to His divinity. The result of the centurion's faith and good attitude was that his servant was healed and his faith was praised as a model for others.

Conclusion

If you think that things can't get worse, don't worry, because at moments like this God hears. Open your heart and turn to Him. Tell Him what you are living and undoubtedly He will work the miracle that you need.

Questions for study and discussion

1. Who were the people who listened to Jesus before this event?

2. What was a centurion?

3. Why did the centurion send Jewish elders to Jesus first?

4. What was the argument the elders used to try convince Jesus to help him?

5. What was the elders' theology as compared to God's answer?

6. Which was the centurion's attitude towards Jesus coming to his house?

7. Which was the centurion's concept of Jesus?

8. Which was Jesus' reaction to the centurion's attitude?

9. How did those who came back find the sick servant?

10. Which is the most outstanding aspect this miracle?

Applicational activities

1. What do you think about yourself? Do you consider yourself as worthy of receiving anything from God?

2. What is your concept of Jesus?

3. How is your faith in Him? Can you describe an event in which He worked a miracle after you had turned to Him?

4. What are the things you need Jesus do for you now? Do you dare ask Him for them right now?

Appetizer for the Soul VIII

✝

The barber

A man went to the barber's to have his hair and beard trimmed. As was usual, he began to chat with the barber, and they talked about different subjects. Eventually, the discussion rolled around to the subject of God. The barber said «I don't think that God exists. All you need is to walk down the street to realize that there is no God. If God existed, why are there so many sick people? Why are there abandoned children? If God existed, there would be no suffering or so much human pain. I can't believe in a God who allows these things to happen.»

The customer sat thinking for a moment, but did not want do answer so as to avoid an argument. The barber finished and the man paid and left the shop. Once he was out, he saw a man walking down the street with long straggly hair and an unkempt beard. The man looked as if he had not visited a barbershop for quite some time.

The next time he went to the barbershop he surprised the barber by saying «Do you know something? Barbers don't exist.» «How is it that barbers don't exist?» asked the barber. «I am a barber and I exist.» «No», said the customer, «They don't exist because if they did, there wouldn't be anyone with long messy hair.» «Well,» said the barber. «If those people came to me they could get their hair cut.» «Exactly!» said the man. «That is precisely the point. God does exist. Yet people don't go to Him nor do they pray to Him; that is why there is so much pain and misery.»11

Chapter Eight

†

Joyful funeral procession

Soon afterward Jesus went with his disciples to the village
of Nain, with a great crowd following him. A funeral procession
was coming out as he approached the village gate. The
boy who had died was the only son of a widow, and many
mourners from the village were with her. When the Lord
saw her, his heart overflowed with compassion. «Don't cry»
he said. Then he walked over the coffin and touched it,
and the bearers stopped. «Young man,» he said «get up.»
Then the dead boy sat up and began to talk to those
around him! And Jesus gave him back to his mother.
Great fear swept the crowd, and they praised God,
saying, «A mighty prophet has risen among us,» and
«we have seen the hand of God at work today.»

The report of what Jesus had done that day spread
all over Judea and even out across its borders.

Luke 7:11-17

I once read about the famous evangelist R.A. Torrey, who during his ministry brought thousands of people to Christ. Before his conversion, he was an unbeliever who left home and his mother's religion. She told him before he left «Son, when you reach the darkest hour of your life and everything seems lost, if you ask your mother's God for help, He will help you.»

Torrey followed his own desires, sinking deeper and deeper in sin, until one day, despondent and without hope, he decided to end his life. In that moment, he remembered his mother's words and, falling on his knees by his bed, said « Oh God of my mother, if you do exist, I ask you to show me Your way.»

The transformation that took place within him after this prayer was admirable. He went on to lead many others to Christ and continues to be a model for the church today.

Luke's story deals with someone that, in the darkest moments in his life, found light in Jesus Christ. We might say that the main theme of this narration is that in Christ there is life and a solution to our problems.

As is fitting with the good doctor Luke, we notice in verse 10 that the translation for «well» is a medical term that means one is completely healed. In verse 15, «sat up» technically means a sick person sitting in his bed.

The story took place in a town called Nain, which was about 40 kilometers southeast of Capernaum. Nain was between Endor and Sunem, where the great prophet Elisha resurrected the son of a Shunammite in 2 kings chapter 4.

Centuries later, history would repeat itself; but this time it was not a prophet but the Son of God who worked the miracle. In some ways, this is one of the most beautiful and tender stories narrated in the Gospel, and we can learn a number of things from it.

Jesus in Nain

Verse 1 says «soon afterwards». That is, the narrative takes place after Jesus had been in Capernaum and had saved a centurion's servant.

Today, we have spiritual advantages that the people of biblical times did not enjoy. For us, Jesus is everywhere at the same time by means of the Holy Spirit. Undoubtedly, at this very moment He is with you and is enjoying your interest in His things. In Zephaniah 3:17, God's word says «The Lord your God is with you, He is mighty to save. He will take great delight in you.»

One of the Gospel's most beautiful truths is that Jesus promised to be with us always until the end of the world. It does not matter how anxious, burdened or sad we might be, Jesus encourages us not to fear or lose heart, for He is with us.

Many think that God is absent or that He is not interested in human affairs. Many have doubted his existence or have even lost their faith. It is possible that the candle of your life is flickering; Jesus wants to fan it into flame it and He has the power to do so. He promised to be with those who search for Him.

The funeral procession

This incident shows us about how painful life can be. In the biblical culture, the funeral procession was led by a group of professional women mourners with flutes and cymbals who cried out piercing screams of sorrow. This particular funeral was very tragic. The expression «the only son of his mother, and she was a widow» condenses a world of pain for the reader.

Virgil, the Roman poet, spoke the immortal words «the tears of the objects» (sunt lacrimae rerum.) This is the nature of things; it is the law of life to live in a world of broken hearts12. Some think that Christianity makes us immune to troubles or sorrow, when Jesus actually never promised us that we would not have any problems. But he did promise that when are walking through the valley of shadow of death He would be with us.

Dear reader, what is the problem, or «coffin» that you are painfully carrying at this moment? In which area of your life is there an area that you don't want to open, see, or touch, one that is slowly leading you to disaster? In John 10:10 God's word says that the devil comes only to steal and kill and destroy. The fact that one belongs to Jesus does not mean that the devil will leave one in peace. On the contrary, he goes on to try and hurt the believer. To be free from the evil intentions of the devil, we must understand that which is hurting us and, with God's help, take biblical steps to free ourselves.

This poor widow was surrounded by friends, neighbors and sympathizers, but few could understand her desperation, her pain. Few could understand her inner grief until, all of a sudden, «the sun of justice with health in his wings» was there for her in the middle of her soul's dark night. I have learned from experience that when God wants to deal with us and take us to greater depths He removes those temporary things that we trust in. He allows us to live through a crisis experience. Whether it be away from be money, family, job or friends, He takes us into a desert and at times might seemingly leaves us alone. He takes away our earthly crutches and leaves us to lean only on Him. Yet after the darkest moments of night, dawn starts breaking. Although your life might seemingly be at this moment in total darkness, you can rely on Christ. Put your faith in him and a hope eternal will spring to life in your soul. God will do something in your life.

Jesus took pity on the woman

In Luke, human tragedy is met by Jesus. The text tells us that He was deeply moved. In Greek, there is no stronger word for pity, sympathy or sensitivity than the one that is used again and again in the Gospel when talking about Jesus´ attitude in these times of trial. Jesus took pity on her.

To the ancient world, this must have been surprising. The noblest faith of antiquity was Stoic. That is, the Stoics believed that God's main characteristic was apathy, a desire not to feel. The Stoics thought that if someone can make another person happy or sad, it means that, at least for a minute, that person can have influence over another. If he can do so, it means that for the briefest of moment he is superior to that person.13 However, no one can be greater than God; therefore, no one can have influence on God. Thus by nature God should be unable to feel. Yet we see here that the Son of God was deeply moved.

Jesus went to the woman and told her «Don't cry.» It does not appear in the story, but it is most probable that as He was moved, some tears would have fallen from His eyes and run down His cheeks as a sign of sorrow for this mother. It was simply the right thing to do.

In the past, death had cruelly stolen his husband, and now, in a coup de grace, it took away her only crutch, her only hope. It took away her beloved son.

In Christ, God would understand her pain as, months later, His eternal tears would fall due to his Son's death on the cross. God still mourns today for the misery of humanity, and wants to give us comfort through Christ.

Our God is not Stoic. He has mercy on each one of us. To us, as with the woman, Jesus is also present. He is the Son of God and died so that we can know God and live an abundant life.

Jesus' compassion was not only expressed in feelings, but in action as well. It gives us pause to think how many times we have expressed compassion only in feelings, but not in practical ways.

Jesus' compassion drove Him to action and He made use of the power given to him the Holy Spirit after His baptism in the River Jordan. In His active compassion we see three aspects.

Jesus went up and touched the coffin

The funeral coffin was not one like ones sold today, but was more a stretcher that carried the body to the tomb. By bringing the youth back to life, Jesus, as a commentator has said «claimed as His own what death had taken as its prey.»14

As the Messiah, Jesus ministered in a way that did not follow Jewish purification laws-he actually touched the corpse of the young man. A person who touched a corpse remained impure for seven days, yet Jesus was showing a more excellent way, and asked for the life of a young man marked by death.

Jesus is not only the Lord of life, but also the Lord over death. He himself triumphed over death and promised that, as He lives, so will the believer.

Christ is the same yesterday, today and forever. He is not only interested in our problems, but is also ready to stand beside us, to walk with us, and to feel our pain and our frustration. No matter how destitute our life may be, He is ready to touch us.

The funeral procession stopped

We can stop and allow Christ to touch us, too. Just as it was out of context for him to touch the body, it might appear odd to others, or even to us, that Christ would want to touch us, that is, meet our needs and have a close relationship with us. Yet scripture tells us that that is what he wants to do. We need to allow Him to do so. Christ was with us as we began this chapter, and He is with us now. Has the time come to allow him to touch you in a closer relationship?

Jesus spoke to her

When the procession stopped Jesus, deeply moved, not only touched the problem but also spoke to the dead youth, saying «Young man, I say to you, get up!» Jesus not only wants to touch the problem, He wants to solve it.

The Word tells us «in repentance and rest is your salvation, in quietness and trust is your strength.» (Isaiah 30:15) It is possible that you already have an ultimate diagnosis. You have come to the end of your rope and there is seemingly no hope. Let me tell you that in Christ there is always hope, that what is impossible for man to see is possible for God to do. The only thing you have to do is stop and give your trouble, your «coffin» to Christ and trust Him, In Jeremiah chapter 29, the prophet says that God has a hope and a future in store for us. God can change adverse circumstances into quietness and peace.

The mother received back her son

The Bible says that the young man was resurrected. Jesus brought him back to life and gave him back to his mother. How could He do so? That day the woman received more than consolation, more than the wise words of a renowned teacher. That day she received her life back.

If we want Jesus to help us with our problem, we first have to give it to Him; we have to halt our «funeral procession», give our problem to Christ and allow Him to declare his Word in our life. Then his miracle will happen.

When he was about to commit suicide, the evangelist Torrey called for his mother's God, and God heard his cry. I do not know what your problem might be. I only know that today Jesus is with you and has compassion for you, that He is by your side and is ready to touch you. I invite you to give your problem to him. Let Him touch you. Let him talk to you. Let Him enact his will and word in your life.

Study guide
Introduction

Summarize the conversion of the evangelist R. A. Torrey.

Transition phrase

At times in one's life the darkest hours precede the dawn. In the story of the widow at Nain, we see that it is true.

Bible reading

Luke 7:11-17

In this narration, as in the former one, Luke the physician tells of Jesus' impact. The story contains at least four important elements

1. Jesus was at Nain

The Bible truth teaches us that God is everywhere at the same moment, that is, He is omnipresent. He is with each believer and wants to do a Nain miracle in our lives, too.

2. There was a funeral procession

This incident shows how painful human life can be. Jesus worked a miracle in the life of a family, going above and beyond what anyone would have imagined. In some way He wants to do the same in our lives, too.

3. Jesus took pity on the woman

Jesus compassion was expressed not only in words, but also in action. Here we see three important aspects: a) Jesus came close to the coffin and touched it. He is ready to touch our problems, too. b) The funeral procession was stopped to make room for a miracle. We must stop so that Jesus might touch us. C) Jesus spoke the youth needed to «hear». Today Christ has just the right word for us, too.

4. The mother received her son

Jesus has something for us to receive, too. What are the «coffins», the problems of our lives that are leading us astray or, even worse, to despondency?

Conclusion

Jesus invites us to give Him our funeral procession, that is, our difficulties. Why not stop and meet Christ right now? He has something for us, too.

Questions for study and discussion

1. When does this miracle occur? Briefly summarize the background.

2. Where was Nain and what other miracle took place there?

3. Why does Luke emphasize the fact that this youth was the only son of the widow?

4. Why did Jesus take pity on her?

5. How did Jesus put his compassion into action?

6. What was Jesus demonstrating by touching a coffin in a culture where to do so caused several days of impurity?

7. What did Jesus do after He touched the coffin?

8. What was the dead young man's reaction when Jesus' spoke?

9. What did Jesus do with the resurrected young man? What does his attitude show?

10. What were some of the results of this miracle story?

Applicational activities

1. Jesus was present at a very important and painful time in this widow's life. What does this imply?

2. Which is the «coffin» or problem that you are carrying now?

3. Are you ready to stop and give Jesus your difficulties?

4. Do you remember an experience in your life where Jesus made a difference? Describe it briefly.

Appetizer for the Soul IX

†

God does not sponsor failures

What does it takes to be a mother? One might suggest responsibility, maturity, good plan planning, etc. Yet simply, to be a mother one must find a father. Now that that fact has been established, I have another question. How do you have a baby?

Time immortal has shown us that both the mother and the father, when conceiving a baby, make a contribution. The mother contributes an egg and the father contributes sperm in which there are spermatozoa.

Now, how many spermatozoa compete to reach the egg? One? Two? Ten? No, millions run the race to get their first. Of those millions, how many fertilize the egg? Half a million? Five? Ten? Simply one gets the job done.

There is no prize for the second place, which means from those millions, just one in a million just gets the privilege of helping create life. Only one is the champion. Only one is the winner. With that one spermatozoon you were created. And like that little guy, God has something for you to do, too. Like our little friend you too are a winner. Why? Simple. God does not sponsor failures.

When the God of life gave you the gift of life, he did it neither by chance, nor by contraceptive failure. He did it because He has a wonderful plan for you. When you say «I am useless, I don't know why I was born, I am the worst, I am trash» you are bringing pain to God because He made you in His own image. God does not make trash. You are a special creation.15

Chapter Nine

†

Spilling the good to be filled with the best

One of the Pharisees asked Jesus to come to his home
for a meal, so Jesus accepted the invitation and sat down to eat.
A certain immoral woman heard he was there and brought a
beautiful jar filled with expensive perfume. Then she knelt
behind him at his feet, weeping. Her tears fell on his feet,
and she wiped them of with her hair. Then she kept
kissing his feet and putting perfume on them. When the
Pharisee who was the host saw what was happening and
who the woman was, he said to himself, «This proves that
Jesus is no prophet. If God had really sent him, he would
know what kind of woman is touching him. She is a sinner.
Then Jesus spoke up and answered his thoughts. «Simon,» he
Said to the Pharisee, «I have something to say to you.» «All
right, Teacher,» Simon replied, «go ahead». The Jesus told
him this story: «A man loaned money to two people, five
hundred pieces of silver to one and fifty pieces to the other.
But neither of them could repay him, so he kindly forgave
them both, canceling their debts. Who do you suppose loved
him more after that?. Simon answered, «I suppose the one for
whom he canceled the larger debt.» «That is right,» Jesus said.
Then he turned to the woman and said to Simon, «Look at
this woman kneeling here. When I entered your home,
You didn't offer me water to wash the dust from my feet,
but she has washed them with her tears and wiped them
with her hair. You didn't give me a kiss of greeting, but

she has kissed my feet again and again from the time

I first came in. You neglected the courtesy of olive oil

to anoint my head, but she has anointed my feet with

rare perfume. I tell you, her sins, and they are many,

have been forgiven, so she has shown me much love.

But a person who is forgiven little shows little love.»

Then Jesus said to the woman, «Your sins are forgiven.»

The men at the table said among themselves, «Who

does this man think he is, going around forgiving sins.»

And Jesus said to the woman, «Your faith has saved

You; go in peace.»

Luke 7:36-50 (See also Matthew 26:6-13 and Mark 14:3-9)

The Argentine singer Sergio Denis sings in one of his songs that if there were no war, peace would not be so appreciated. The universe itself consists of contrasts. We have light and darkness, happiness and sadness, life and death, etc. Many spiritual truths are better understood on the basis of contrasts and Jesus, the master teacher, frequently used this method in his teachings.

In this chapter we will focus on two people who viewed Christ differently. I hope that through it you will understand that God wants you to pour out your heart before Him as a sign of dependence on Him. If we are humble before Him we will be open to receive His blessing. We will see that a real encounter with Jesus is transforming in every sense.

In the passage we notice three groups of people. We have Jesus, who represents God's eternal and forgiving love, we have a group of Pharisees lead by Simon, representing those considering themselves as just before God, and we also have the sinful woman, who represents all those admitting their need for God. The whole episode is presented as an act in three scenes:

a) The supper with Simon, the rest of the Pharisees and the sinful woman.

b) Jesus' dialogue with the Pharisees.

c) Jesus' dialogue with the sinful woman and the conclusion of the story.

This story is so vivid that it seems as if Luke could have been a natural writer. The whole episode takes place at Simon's house. The house, as was customary of Simon's economic class, was built around a square yard that contained a garden and fountain. When the weather was hot meals were served in the garden. In this culture, when a rabbi had dinner at someone's house all kinds of people would gather to hear his wisdom. This explains the woman's presence. In that culture people did not sit at the table but rather sat on low couches around it, leaning on it with their left elbow, with their feet back and leaving their right arm free. During meals they took off their sandals. This explains why the woman could be kneeling at Jesus' feet.

It is interesting that Simon would have invited Jesus to his house.

Why would he have done this? There are three possible answers:

a) He did it because he was an admirer of Jesus, as not all the Pharisees were Jesus' enemies. However, it did remain unusual that a Pharisee would do this.

b) He did it because he intended to lay a trap for Jesus, to have something to accuse him of. However, he did treat Jesus with respect, calling him Rabbi.

c) Most probably Simon enjoyed having celebrities to his house and with this in mind he invited this young Galilean to have dinner with him. This explains the strange combination that combines a certain amount of respect with a certain lack of politeness required on this occasion.

The story is a contrast between two attitudes: one of skepticism and one of acceptance. Here we see various marked differences between the Pharisees and the sinful woman masterfully shown by Jesus in such a way that the reader can understand the point of the story.

Self justice vs. Need

As a Pharisee, Simon was plagued by a self-sufficiency that kept him from acknowledging his need for Christ. Basing his relationship with God more on maintaining strict stipulations than on accepting grace, he stood in contrast to the woman who, kneeling at Christ's feet, accepted grace with pain and joy.

Self-sufficiency closes the door between man and God, yet, in an odd way, the better a man thinks he is, the more he might feel his sin. Paul could speak for man sinful men when he said about sinners «...of whom I am the worst.» Saint Francis would say that there was no sinner more depraved and miserable than himself.

Perhaps the greatest sin is not to be aware of one's sin. Doing this lessens our need for God. How big is our love for Christ? If we love God just a little, could it be that we think that we are too good and that we really don't need Him?

Hypocrisy vs. Honesty

Jesus knew what Simon was thinking about the woman and said to him «Simon, I have something to tell you.» Simon answered, «Tell me, teacher.»

Here we see Simon's hypocrisy. He verbally recognized Jesus as a teacher, but his heart was far from his teaching.

On many occasions, we behave in the same way. We sing, we pray and proclaim Jesus as our Lord and yet do not live the Gospel as we should. This is hypocrisy. The woman had a notorious reputation. She was a prostitute.

Undoubtedly, she had seen Jesus talking to the multitudes and she saw in Him the help needed to lift her up from the miry clay of her life. She was vulnerable and admitted her need and threw herself at Jesus feet. She knew she had nothing to offer Him and that she needed His forgiveness. This is the attitude that God wants to find within us.

Rejection vs. Welcome

At the time of the story, roads were primitive and shoes were sandals consisting of soles tied by straps that crossed the feet. Thus, it was customary to pour fresh water on a guest's feet to clean and refresh them as a sign of welcome.

Yet Simon the Pharisee did not follow this ritual of welcome with Jesus. Nevertheless, the woman washed his feet and then dried them with her hair. What was scandalous was not only what the woman did, but how she did it. By drying Jesus' feet with her hair it had to have been loose. A Jewish woman of that time who let her hair hang down portrayed a lack of modesty.

In fact, when a Jewish woman married she wore her hair tied up and did not wear it loose again. The fact that she wore her hair down in front of others shows how she moved beyond social expectations in order to meet Jesus.

Most probably her tears were abundant and the text says that she to «wet his feet with her tears». When Jesus was at Nain with the widow who had lost her only son, he told her not to cry. He did not say the same to the prostitute, but allowed her to mourn her life of sin and gain freedom from it.

For years, this poor woman, this sinner, had repressed her pain, her shame, her sin and her frustration; but now, she found herself before a man who was different and before whom she could cry openly. We might say that each tear running down onto Jesus' feet represented a sin in her life. On another occasion Jesus said, «Blessed those who mourn for they will be comforted.» This truth was a reality in the life of this woman.

When was the last time you cried tears of repentance, aware of your need before Jesus? Most of our spiritual harshness is due to the fact that we are not aware of the pain our sins have caused God. Our tears or repentance are the beginning of comfort and restoration.

Indifference vs. Friendship

At that time, the host also would lay his hand on the guest's shoulder and give him a kiss as a sign of peace and friendship. It was a sign of respect that was never omitted when one had a distinguished rabbi to dinner. But Simon did not do that. It was obvious from the context that Simon invited Jesus to dinner but did not treat him with the respect He deserved. Though not portrayed as antagonistic to Christ, but he certainly was not devoted to him. Nevertheless, this sinful woman was devoted to Jesus and not only washed his feet with her tears and dried them with her hair, but also kissed them tirelessly. We see in the story a beautiful picture of redemption. We are Jesus' friends and He is ours and we must obey Him. And thatmfriendship must be developed by means of a daily personal relationship in which we adore him in worship and grow in grace.

Apathy vs. High esteem

Culturally, the host would also pour some oil or rose water over the guest's head or burn some incense as a symbol of esteem. As a sign of acceptance and manners, all those things would need to be accomplished, yet this did not happen to Simon and Jesus.

Simon did not pour oil or rose water over Jesus' head to show Christ recognition. Most probably he felt superior to Jesus. Verse 39 says that he knew who that woman was, but did not think that Jesus did. The woman, as did many women at that time, had a perfume bottle tied to her neck. This perfume was alabaster and was expensive, probably costing a year's savings.

The woman wanted to pour it on his feet because it was all she had to offer, but on seeing him she cried and fell in repentance and worship.

There she opened the perfume bottle and poured it over Jesus' feet, knowing that He was worth much more. It was the only pure thing she had to offer, because everything else in her life was contaminated by sin.

Damnation vs. Forgiveness

The Pharisee understood the lesson but in the story he did not change his attitude. However, the woman experienced forgiveness from all her sins. She heard Jesus telling her that her sins were forgiven. From that day on she was somebody new. The weight of her sins was taken away and for the first time, she experienced real peace. The dark corners of her heart were whiter than snow through Jesus' forgiveness.

Criticism vs. Salvation

The Pharisees, led by Simon, surely began to criticize and question Jesus when told the woman «Your faith has saved you; go in peace.»

She not only experienced the forgiveness of her sins but also received from Jesus the gift of eternal life, the certainty of salvation.

When dealing with God's works we are confronted with contrasting attitudes: criticism and doubt or humility and acceptance. Who will be our model, Simon the Pharisee or the sinful woman? Maybe you have nothing to offer God at this moment. Maybe you are tired, exhausted or burdened with troubles, and most likely you don't have a year's worth of savings to give Him. Yet let me tell you that you have something even more valuable that Jesus is waiting for you to give.

Pour out your heart before God as if it were a rich alabaster perfume. Renew your covenant with Him; tell Him what you need, that you wish to follow Him to the end. If you want to cry before him, do that freely; it does not matter what people might say, or who might be around. God wants you to yield to Him as your Lord, and give Him everything. He wants to say to you what he said to the woman «Your faith has saved you; go in peace.» What are you going to do with Jesus' invitation?

Study guide
Introduction

Life consists of contrasts: grief and joy, peace and war, love and hate, etc.

Transitional phrase

For this study we will meditate on the life of two people who viewed Christ differently.

Bible reading

Luke 7:36-50; Mathew 26:6-13 and Mark 14:3-9

We could divide the whole story in three scenes: Jesus' dinner with Simon, the Pharisees and the rest of the guests; Jesus' dialogue with Simon and, finally, Jesus' dialogue with the sinful woman. In this story we see the following contrasts:

Self-Justice vs. Need

Self-sufficiency shuts the door between God and men.

Hypocrisy vs. Honesty

We refer to Jesus as the Master, but often we do what we want and thus practice hypocrisy. God wants to both heal and protect us from this, and recognizing this sin in our lives is the first step towards freedom.

Rejection vs. Welcome

God does not reject a contrite and humble heart. When we approach Jesus as the woman did, He receives us as well.

Indifference vs. Friendship

The believer is the friend of Jesus, and this friendship is shown by obedience to him. It is possible to be a believer yet be indifferent to the heart of God. When this happens we need to ask forgiveness at the feet of our Lord.

Apathy vs. High esteem

The woman poured a year's savings on Jesus feet. What do we need to do to show Christ that He is Lord?

Condemnation vs. forgiveness

The Pharisee kept the same attitude he had of Jesus and did not receive forgiveness, yet the woman knew her sins, sought forgiveness, and received it.

Criticism vs. Salvation

The Pharisees began to criticize and question Jesus, but the woman received salvation and forgiveness. What would our attitude be?

Conclusion

God expects us to «pour out» to him that which is valuable to us. He wants us to give it to him as the woman did.

Questions for study and discussion

1. Why did Jesus go to dine to the Pharisee's house?

2. How were sinful woman viewed in Jesus' time?

3. How do we know that the alabaster bottle was costly?

4. Why did Jesus tell Simon the story of the two debtors?

5. What are the main points that Jesus wants to teach with this story?

6. What did the oil on the head, the water for the feet and the kiss represent in Jesus' day?

7. Which was Simon's reaction to Jesus' lesson?

8. What happened to the sinful woman? What did Jesus give her?

9. What were the people's reactions to the gift of forgiveness given by Jesus to the woman?

Applicational Activities

1. How much love do I have for Jesus?

2. How do I express my love for Jesus?

3. Have you had an experience with the Lord like that of the woman? Describe it

4. What is your attitude towards other sinners? Do you forgive generously?

Appetizer for the Soul X

†

Roses for Valentine's Day

He had died a year ago and an important date was comming. On Valentine's day, every year he would send her a bunch of roses with a card saying: "I love you more than last year. My love will keep on growing year after year". But this was the first time Rose would not get them. She was missing them, when somebody knocked at the door and, to her surprise, when she opened it, there was a bunch of roses before her with a card that said: "I love you". Of coures she was upset, thinking that it was a bad joke. She phoned the flower shop immediately, to complain about what had happened. The owner picked up the phone. He told her that he was aware that her husband had died over a year ago and he asked her if she had read the card. Then he explained that her husband had paid for the roses in advance, so that she would be getting them for the rest of her life.

When Rose put down the receiver, she was in tears. When she opened the card that was written by her husband, it said: "Hello, my love. I know this was a very hard year for you. I expect you to recover soon, but I just wanted to tell you that I will love you forever and that we will be together again. Roses will be sent to you every year. The day that you don't answer the door, they will try five times to find you, and if you are not there, they will be sure to send them where you will be, next to me. Love, your husband."

If a person is capable of loving so much, how are we not going to love God more, who day by day shows us His immense love, and with whom we'll be· together someday?16

Chapter Ten

†

The defeated giant

So they arrived in the land of the Gerasenes, across
the lake from Galilee. As Jesus was climbing out of the
boat, a man who was possessed by demons come out
to meet him. Homeless and naked, he had lived in a cementery
for a long time. As soon as he saw Jesus, he striked and fell to
the gournd before him, screaming, "Why are you bothering me,
Jesus, Son of the Most High God? Please, I beg you, don't torture
Me!" For Jesus had already commanded the evil spirit to come
out of him. This spirit had often taken control of the man.
Even when he was shackled with chains, he simply broke them
and rushed out into the wilderness, completely under the demon's
power. "What is your name?" Jesus asked. "Legion," he replied,
for the man was filled with many demons. The demons kept
begging Jesus not to send them into the Bottomless Pit. A large
herd of pigs was feeding on the hillside nearby, and the demons
pleaded whit him to let them enter into the pigs. Jesus gave them
permission. So the demons came out of the man and entered
the piga, and the whole herd plunged down the steep hillside into
the lake, where they drowned. When the herdsmen saw it, they
fled to the nearby city and the sorrounding countryside, spreading
the news as they ran. A crowd soon gathered around Jesus,
for they wanted to see for themselves what had happened.
And they saw the man who hadd been possessed by demons
Sitting quietly at Jesus'feet, clothed and sane. And the whole

Crowd was afraid. Then those who had seen what happened told the others how the demonpossessed man had been healed. And all the people in that region begged Jesus to go away and leave them alone, for a great wave of fear swept over them. So Jesus returned to the boat and left, crossing back to the other side of the lake. The man who had been demon possessed begged to go, too, but Jesus said, "No, go back to your family and tell them all the wonderfull things God has done for you." So he went all through the city telling about the grat thing Jesus had done for him.

Luke 8:26-39 (See also Matthew 8:28-34 and Mark 5:1-17)

Many years ago, while I was still a student at the Buenos Aires Bible Institute, I was leading a youth group in a suburbian church, together with another fellow student. Suddenly, a young man came to us. He was about eighteen, he looked haggard and very scared, because he had escaped from an "umbanda" center, which is an Afro-Brasilian satanic cult.. He wanted us to help him.

My fellow student and I took him to a separate room. After talking for a while and presenting the Gospel of Christ to him, we started to pray, casting out the torturing demons who referred to themselves with the names of saints.I should say it wasn't a very nice scene, but at that moment, I realized the authority that I had in Christ's name over people with demonic problems. Since that experience, God has put me in situations in which I have been able to see His power and authority at my disposal.

Luke's story talks about the experience of a young man in the Bible, who was totally posessed by demons, but by meeting Jesus he had been transformed and was freed. The purpose of this chapter is that you, my dear reader, may understand that, as Christians who belong to Christ's Church, we have authority to overcome Satan in the name of Christ, just as David could defeat the giant Goliath. We will never understand this story if we do not bear in mind that, no matter what we think about demons, they were absolutely real to the Gerasenes and to the young man whose mind was seriously disturbed. To understand this story, we must be aware that Satan is a real being and that he is now working as he did in the past. To many Christians this narration may be symbolic, others might say that just a structure of society is demonic but that demons are not real and intelligent beings. To understand the essence of this message, we must consider that the demons are fallen angels with intelligence and will.

This is an extreme case, the young man lost his mind. It is one of the few occasions wherethe expression "possessed by demons" is used. Nowadays, psychiatrists would have diagnosed multilpe and chronic schizophrenia and they would have sent him to to a rehabilitation institute. But in those days, as there were no such institutes, he was sent to the tombs or caves, for they were considered to be the place for demons.

Satan works in three different ways in a person, but with the same purpose. Externally: by means of pressure through sickness, financial problems, family problems, etc. Internally: through bondages of non-resolved sins, negative experiences of the past, etc. And, demonizations: through the practice of sin, by turning to witch doctors, spiritualists or clarivoyants, etc.

If Christ is the Lord of our life, we will never be objects of demonization or bondage, only of pressure. But if Christ is not the Lord of our life, we are the perfect target for any of these. The key to freedom is to surrender each area of our life to Jesus' domain. It is not enough to be saved. We need to surrender each area of our life to be under Jesus' rule, each «room» of our being to be given over to the Holy Spirit. The devil`s purpose is to control our mind, and he uses any method to reach this goal.

But the wonderful thing is that in Christ, we have authority and power to break any bondage or to get rid of any pressure or demon. The experience of this youg man illustrates for us some steps to freedom:

Jesus confronted the young man

When Jesus left the boat and saw this young man, He began to order the demons inside him to leave. When Jesus ordered his disciples to preach the Gospel, he said: *"And these signs will accompany those who believe: In my name they will drive out demons"* (Mark 16-17). Mathew says that we are granted all authority from Jesus. Paul says that all things are submitted to Christ, who is the head of the church.

Therefore, each one of us individually and as the Body of Christ haveauthority against all diabolical power in the name of Jesus and through

His blood. Many Christians are living as if they were defeated because they have not been completely freed. As leaders, we have to take charge of the matter. Nowadays, God has given us weapons like intercession, liberation, inner healing, etc. in order to help the members in our congregations to live the abundant life that Jesus wants to give them.

The demons reacted before Jesus' authority

In this case, there is a main demon with a group of other demons of less category. Since long ago, they were strongly attacking this young man. They exerted such violence against him that they could not have him still even in chains.

When Jesus confronted them, they recognized Jesus as the Son of God Almighty. How did they know? The just presence of Christ got them anxious; but the answer might be that thousands of years ago, those same demons had been with Christ in the glory of God Almighty. They had been on the same side before, but now they were God's archenemy.

The devil has already been defeated by Christ, but his fall is progressive. It is like a soccer game between a good team and a bad one. The bad team knows before hand that he has alrready been beated, but their fall becomes more and more obvious as goals are made against them. The fall of Satan can be seen with three resounding goals from God.

From heaven

Isaiah 14:12 says: "How have you fallen from heaven, o morning star, son of dawn! You have been cast down to the earth, you who once laid low the nations." Satan was formerly called Lucifer and was in charge of supervising God's creation. But, due to his pride and arrogance, because he wanted to be the same as God, he was thrown from Heaven to hell together with the third part of the angels. Hell was created by God for Satan and his demons. This is the first one God put over Satan: He threw him out of His presence. God lives no longer with Satan and his demons. Though for some reason Satan still has access to God, there will come a day when this access will stop.

From earth

Genesis 1:1,2 says: "In the beginning God created the heavens and the earth. Now the earth was formless and empty, darkness was over the surface of the deep…" In verse 3 we see how the light was created, that is, how God started to fill the earth He had created before. Millions of years could have passed between verse 2 and 3. When Satan was thrown from heaven to hell, he went out of there and came to earth, which God had created long ago.

This explains why the earth was empty, in disorder and in darkness. God is a God of order and where He is there is no emptiness. His presence is light. This is how Satan came to earth.

When God created Adan and Eve, He gave them the ownership of the planet, but when they disobeyed, they gave it to the devil and, since then, he has been the legal owner. But when Jesus died on the cross, He recovered the title and He was then the new, true and eternal owner of the earth. Satan is an intruder. He left the earth as his headquarters, and settled in the air, wherefrom he tries to harm God's creation.

But on Jesus' second coming, Satan will be definitely destroyed, and by a thousand years he will be tied up, and then he will be thrown to hell where he will remain through eternity. This is the second goal scored by God.

From the air

Ephesians 6:12 says: "For our struggle is not against flesh and blood, but against the rulers, against the authorities against the powers of this dark world and against the spiritual forces of evil in the heavenly realms." Now Satan's centre of operations is in the air, in the heavenly realms. He was thrown from heaven by God and he will also be thrown from the air by Christ and his church. When we will be captured in the air with Christ, then Satan will be definitely expelled from there too. That will be the third and efinite goal scored by God.

He was thrown from heaven because the glory of God filled that place, and he will be trown from earth and from the air because the glory of God will fill those places with His presence, as the waters cover the sea. What does this mean? It simply means that where God is, there is no more room for anybody else. If Christ fills my life, then there is no more room for anything or anybody else.

That is why when Christ came to Gadara, the demons who were in the young man reacted against Jesus. This means that, every time a son of God is aware of his position in Christ and exerts his authority in Him, demons will react. But they do not leave easely, it is necessary that we expell them.

God lives in His people's praises and this is somathing that the devil does not resist and he becomes restless. Moreover, Christ said that his church is built over Him and that the doors of hell wil not prevail against His church (Mathew 16:18).

When Jeus asked the devil what his name was, he told Him: Legion. On those days, a legion represented an army of 6.000 Roman soldiers. This means that this man was possessed by a multitude of demons with a leader. When they saw Christ, they begged Him not to send them to hell.

Here we see Jesus sovereignty over the demons, who begged Him please, not to send them to hell. When we personally and as a church we assume the authority we have in Christ, the demons begin to react and to tremble.

The man was freed. It is not enough to have authority, we ust exert it. A public authority, as a policeman, apart from his uniform, he has a whistle. In case of emergency or need, the policeman an stand up in the middle of the road, or raise up his hand or blow his whistle to stop a big truck. Of course, the truck is stronger than the policeman, but the policeman has much more authority. Thus, Jesus told us that, if we believe, this would be one of the signals that would come with our job of preaching; weeould have authority over demons. This young man was completely freed, but after Jesus ordered the demons to leave.

The text tells us that the young man was then sitting at Jesus feet, well dressed and in his right mind. We do not know why Jesus allowed that demons to get into the pigs who were eating nearby; the only thing we can be sure of is that one life is worth more than anything.

The demonizations, the bondages and the Satanic oppressions takes us our peace away together with our emotional stability; but when we are freed through Jesus' truth, we then experiment serenity and the true peace that exceedes all human understanding, that is, we are in our right mind.

End results

There were two kinds of reactions:

a) The Gerasenes, who asked Jesus to leave. They hated any alteration in their lives routine. They were eaceful up to that moment; but now Jesus had come to bother them and so they wanted Him to leave.

Nowadays, many people hate Jesus because His sanctity bothers them; they do not want Jesus to point at their sins. Many people in our community are happy because we develop our activities within our churches, but when we go out and start to talk about Jesus, to say who Christ is and what He expects from us, we see how they lose patience and they begin to hate us. The Gerasenes loved their pigs much more than the young man's life. One of the dangers we always run is to appreciate things more than people, programs rather than persons.

b) There was the man that was healed. He wanted to follow Jesus, but He sent him bach home. Christian testimony, as well as Christian charity and good manners, start at home first. It is easier to talk about Christ to people that we do not know; but our duty is to testify in the place Christ put us in. It has been many years since my first experience with a person possessed by a demon, but day after day I believe more and more in the authority that we have in Christ as Christians. Dear reader, no matter what you problem might be now, no matter if the devil is attacking you with oppressions, bondages or possessions. We have and we believe in Christ who has already defeated Satan and has given us that same power and authority.

Therefore, if at this moment you are going through any difficulty related to the world of darkness, I suggest that you look for the help of a reliable person. But in the meantime, I encourage you to say aloud the following prayer:

Lord Jesus, at this moment, as your church, as your body and in your authority, we face every evil spirit and in your name we bond it and declare him ineffective and we throw him away. And with the same authority that you delayed in us, we open the doors of heaven so that your power may be shown in our lives and so that you may fill our hearts with your Spirit each and every day. Thank you, Father, for your presence and for the victory You have given us. In Jesus' name. Amen.

Study guide
Introduction

Make a brief summary on a personal experience or someone else's, in which you have seen God's power.

Transitional phrase

There was once a man who was totally possessed by demons, but a personal encounter with Jesus transformed him and freed him completely.

Bible reading

Luke 8:26-39; Mathew 8:28-34 and Mark 5:1-17

In order to understand this story, it is essential that we believe that Satan is a real being and that, nowadays he is still working, as in the past. In this story we can see, some steps to free this young man.

1. Jesus faced the young man

When Jesus stepped ashore and saw the young man, he came to him and He did not evade him. We need to learn how to help people that are struggling with spiritual problems of this nature.

2. The demons reacted before Jesus' authority

When Jesus comes near, the demons start to scream. When we live filled with the Holy Spirit and in sanctity, the enemy does not resist our presence. We must remember that Satan has already been defeated and thrown away. A) From heaven: Isaiah 14:12; B) From earth: Genesis 1:1-3; C) From the air: Ephesians 6:12

3. The young man was freed

It is not enough to have authority. We need to exercise it. In Christ we can be free and free others.

4. End results

a)   The Gerasenes wanted Jesus to leave their place.

b)   The young man who was freed wanted to follow Jesus.

Conclusion

It does not matter that the enemy may attack us with oppressions, bondages or possessions. In Christ we can be free.

Questions for study and discussion

1. Where was the region of the Gerasenes? Was it part of Israel?

2. How was the young man when he met Jesus?

3. Which was the young man's reaction when he saw Jesus?

4. Why did the young man react in this way?

5. Why did Jesus have started to talk to the devils?

6. What does show about Jesus the fact that the demons asked Him a favour?

7. When was the young man freed? Where were the devils gone to?

8. What was the local people's reaction when they knew what had happened?

9. What was the freed young man's reaction once he was in his right mind?

10. What did Jesus ask the young man to do?

Applicational activities

1. Summarize an experience in which you were able to see God's liberating power in your life.

2. Are you affraid to get into the spiritual world of demons, to help people with such problems? If your answer is yes or no, why?

3. Do you have now any spiritual struggle in which you need especially Jesus' help?

4. If you have experienced God's power in your life, what are you doing in that respect? Have you told it to other people as a testimony?

Appetizer for the Soul XI

†

The Geese

Next season, when you see geese migrating to a warmer place to spend the winter, just check if they fly in V-formation. You may be interested to know why they do so.

It is because when they flap their wings, each bird produces an air movement that helps the bird behind it. Flying in V, the flock increases their power of flight by 71%, as compared with a single bird flyng on his own. People who share a common goal and who have a sense of community, can accomplish their goals more easily and quickly, because of their mutual support, which betters their achievements.

Each time that a goose leaves the formation, it feels immediately the air resistance, and it realizes how difficult it is to fly alone and quickly gets back to the formation to benefit form the partner who flies in front of it. If we get together and stay with those who are going in the same direction, the achieving of our goals is less strenuous, simpler and even more pleasant.

When the leader of the geese gets tired, it goes to the back and another goose takes its place. We men will obtain better results if we support each other in the bad moments, if we respect each other and if we always share our problems and our most difficult tasks.

The geese who fly in the back honk to encourage those in the front to keep their speed. A timely word of hope is of great help, gives strength, motivates and produces great benefits.

Finally, when a goose gets shot and spirals downward, two other geese leave the formation and follow it in order to give it their support and protection, untill it recovers. If the wounded goose dies, the two supportive geese go back to their formation. In the same way, if we stay together, supporting each other and keeping each other company, if we show real team spirit, and if, in spite of our differences, we can form a group of human beings that can face all kinds of situations, if we understand the true meaning of friendship and brotherhood, if we are aware of the feeling of sharing, then life will be simpler and time will be more pleasant as the years fly by17.

Chapter Eleven

†

From Suffering to Happines

On the other side of the lake the crowds received Jesus with open arms because they had been waiting for him. And now a man named Jairus, a leader of the local synagogue, came and fell down at Jesus' feet, begging him to come home with him. His only child was dying, a little girl twelve years old. As Jesus went with him, he was surrounded by the crowds.

While he was still speaking to a woman, a messenger arrived from Jairus's home with the message, "Your little girl is dead. There's no use troubling the Teacher now." But when Jesus heard what had happened, he said to Jairus, "Don't be afraid. Just trust me, and she will be all right." When they arrived at the house, Jesus wouldn't let anyone go in with him except Peter, James, John, and the little girl's father and mother. The house was filled with people weeping and wailing, but he said, "Stop the weeping! She isn't dead, she is only asleep." But the crowd laughed at him because they all knew she had died. Then Jesus took her by the hand and said in a loud voice, "Get up, my child!" And at that moment her life returned, and she immediately stood up! Then Jesus told them to give her something to eat. Her parents were overwhelmed, but Jesus insisted that they not tell anyone what had happened.

Luke 8:40-42, 49-56 (See also Matthew 9:18-26 and Mark 5:22-43)

Many years ago in the church, chidren sang a very nice song that said: "With Christ in the family, what a happy home, what a happy home, what a happy home!"

Nowadays, we live in a time where the image of home has been greatly deteriorated, where the problems have overstrained the strength of the family members and their collapse is imminent. Due to social changes, especially in Latin America, parents must spend more time away from home because of their job. We must also consider that in certain religious circles, those parents spend many nights per week in different ministries. The outlook is not very hopeful, but it is necessary that we remember that with Christ in our family we can have a peaceful home, not without problems, but with wisdom to solve them.

I now invite you to meditate on the story of a family consisting of a couple whose only child that had died. We will see what the father did to solve this problem, so that we may know who to turn to in our difficulties.

In this story, told by the three evangelists, we find that all of a sudden, all the suffering of life turns into joy. Luke was deeply moved by the death of this girl, because he adds a little more suspense to the passage. Undoubtedly, Jairus, his daughter and Jesus are the main characters in the story, which gives us three basic elements:

There is a man in need

As a good physician and historian, Luke gives us details about Jairus. This man was the head or president of the synagogue. In Israel, the synagogues were the educational extension centers for the temple of Jerusalem; they taught doctrine to the Jewish men and they were schools for the boys.

Jairus was in charge of the administration of the synagogues and of the public sabbatical service. He had reached the highest post that life could give him in the eyes of his fellow citizens. He was obviously of a very high social standing, and he had climbed the ladder of wordly ambition and prestige. It appeared that life had been very favorable to him but now it was about to rob him of his most precious belonging.

The background of the story consists of all the suffering of life, which we know too well, because we also live in a world with very much grief. The professional crying women had already come. We can think of them as repulsively false, but in Palestine they hired these women to show respect for the dead, a custom which was never omitted. As the story goes, Jairus fell down at Jesus' feet, asking him to go to his house, because his only daughter, who was twelve, was about to die.

This is dreadful. The scene showed Jairus' deep need. The child who lights up their life was dying. The girl was about twelve; therefore, she was about to become an adult, for in the East, and in those times, children assumed responsibilities earlier than in the West. At that age she could have been ready to marry. What should have been the dawn of her life was full of darkness. Those of us who are parents and who have gone through the sickness of a child can understand Jairus' desperation. A child changes our priorities and our scale of values. When we truly love our children, we would sacrifice anything for their good. Having to watch them suffer makes us desperate. This is how Jairus felt when he went to see Jesus.

Jairus turns to Jesus through his need

Jairus, a desperate family man, went to Jesus and invited Him to go to his house. Jairus was a man who could have been too proud to turn to Jesus. He was the sinagogue ruler. Most probably, the doors of of the sinagogue at Capernaum where Jairus lived- were closed to Jesus' ministry at that moment.

Jairus belonged to that kind of people that generally rejected Jesus' ministry; but the serious illness of his only daugther of twelve made him look for His help. He might have hated Jesus and considered Him a transgressor of the law. But in his time of need, he swallowed his pride and asked for His help.

There is a famous story of Roland, Charlemagne's paladin. He was in charge of the army's rearguard. One day, in the middle of the battle, he was attacked by his enemies. Roland carried with him a horn, called Olivant, which could be heard within a radius of 45 kilometers. According to the story, it was so powerful that the birds would drop dead when its sound penetrated the air. His friend begged him to blow the horn so that Charlemagne could hear it and come to his rescue. But Roland was too proud. One by one his men died in combat, until he was the only one who remained. In the end, with his last breath he blew the horn, and when Charlemagne heard it he came as fast as he could. But it was too late for Roland was already dead. He had been too proud to ask for help.

It is easy to proceed in this way: to think that we can work things out by ourselves. But the only way to find God's gracious miracles is to set our pride aside, to humbly confess our need and to ask for God's help. Jeus says: "Ask and it will be given." But we do not receive without asking first. No matter what your social standing might be now, if you have a need, set your pride aside, turn to Jesus and give your problem to him.

Jairus was discouraged by the people

The story says that while Jesus went to Jairus' house, the crowd almost crushed him, so his progresswas slow. Moreover, as he was making his request of Jesus, another miracle was performed: a woman who was subject to bleeding was healed. So He was apparently wasting His precious time. Suddenly, someone came to Jairus and told him not to bother Jesus anymore for his daughter was dead.

There will always be people, friends, relatives, circumstances, etc. telling us in words or attitudes: "Don't turn to Jesus, don't go on being a Christian. Jesus can't help you anyway, you have to solve it yourself. Your situation is so terrible that nothing can change it."

Let me remind you that, notwithstanding the magnitude of your problem, there is always hope in Christ. What is impossible for man, is possible with God. I was told that in a small congregation a young man was once converted to Christianity; he worked and testified of Jesus with great love and courage. One of the leaders told the other: "Have you seen that young man? He's so enthusiastic and hard working!" The other leader answered: "Don't worry, it's not gonna' last." There will always be people as in Nehemiahs' time, who will want to discourage us, so we need to be wiser and more determined in order to overcome it.

Jesus dealt with his problem

While others told Jairus not to bother the teacher any more, Jesus told Jairus: "Don't be afraid; just believe and she will be healed." Fear paralyzes us and skepticism hinders God's work. That is why Jesus told him: "Don't be afraid; just believe". That is to say, trust God and He will do His work.

Jairus was a man of tenacious faith. No matter what he felt or heard, he was not willing to accept the verdict of the crying women. He went home with Jesus and went into the girl's room together with Peter, James and John, Jesus' disciples.

He believed that something would happen. He believed against all lost hope. Undoubtedly, in his heart he had this unspoken feeling: "You never know what Jesus can do." And none of us knows for sure what Jesus may do. In the darkest day we can trust in the remotest riches, in the immense grace and in the unbeatable power of God. It is said that only after the darkest hours of the night does dawn start to break.

Once inside the room, Jesus stopped the crying, He kneeled by the girl's bed, He took her hand and with tenderness and authority he said: "My child, get up." Immediately, Death obeyed the Author of Life and gave back what it had previously wanted to steal. Then Jesus told them to give her something to eat, thus showing that she was really alive and, why not, letting her parents relax a little and have something to eat too after so many hours of pain and shadows. What a teacher Jesus is! He is in every detail, taking care not only of the child but also of her parents; responding not only to a specific need, such as giving life to a dead person, but also bringing peace and tranquillity to lives in distress.

What is the difficulty that you are facing now? In this very moment, I urge you to invite Jesus into your heart and into your home, as Jairus did. When Jesus comes to your heart and you take Him as your Lord and Savior, He will start to calm your anxiety and solve your problems.

I invite you to give your problem to God. Don't do as Roland, Charlemagne's paladin, who died because he did not ask for help due to his pride. In this moment, blow your prayer horn and raise your petition to God.

Let's learn from Jairus, who being Jesus' advesary, turned to Him calling for help in the darkest hour of his life. Give your need to Jesus right now and the miracle will be performed for your own good and for God's glory.

Study Guide
Introduction

Write a brief summary of a story in which you have seen Jesus working in a very special way.

Transitional Phrase

In the most difficult moments we must turn to the right person, that is, to Jesus, in order to solve our problems.

Bible Reading

Luke 8:40-42, 49-56; Mathew 9:18-26 and Mark 5:22-43

In this story we find that all the pfamily's grief suddenly turns to joy. We find four important elements in this story:

1. There is a man in need

Jairus, as the sinagogue ruler, had attained a very high social standing; but it was of no use in times like this. He decided to set his pride aside and turn to Jesus for help.

2. Jairus turns to Jesus with his need

Tell briefly the story of Roland, one of Charlemagne's paladins. Jairus belonged to a class of people that could possibly reject Jesus' ministry, but in a moment of deep necessity, he turned to Him.

3. There was discouragement

There will always be people, friends or relatives that by their words or attitudes will tell us not to turn to Jesus. We should never forget, that no matter how big our problem may be, there is always hope in Jesus.

4. Jesus deals with your problem

While the rest discouraged Jairus, Jesus encouraged him to believe and not to be afraid. He took three of His disciples, went to his house and resurrected Jairus' daughter.

Conclusion

We will never know what Jesus may do. Basically, faith is a space in our minds and hearts for Jesus to surprise us. If there is something that you may find impossible, give it to Jesus and He will do it.

Questions for Study and Discussion

1. Where had Jesus been before this incident?

2. What was a synagogue ruler?

3. Why does Luke give more details on Jairus and his daughter?

4. What was Jesus' answer when He heard the people telling Jairus not to bother Him because the girl had already died?

5. What were Jairus' feelings when he heard the news?

6. Why did Jesus take only three of his disciples with Him?

7. What was the people's response when Jesus told them that the girl was asleep?

8. What did Jesus do to the girl?

9. What was the girl's response to Jesus' order?

10. What was her parent's reaction to the miracle of life?

Appicational Activities

1. If you were to present only one petition to Jesus, what would it be?

2. What are your human resources that could fulfill such a petition?

3. What is the price you have to pay so that Jesus may take His place in your situation?

4. Do you believe Jesus can help you? If your answer is positive, don't lose any more time. Seek Jesus earnestly and desperately, as Jairus did.

Appetizer for the Soul XII

†

A ring to my mother

The boy walked purposefully into the jewelry store and he asked the owner to show him the best engagement ring he had. The jeweler showed him one. The beautiful solitarie shined like a tiny gleaming sun. The boy looked at the ring and he smiled in approval. Then he asked for its price and he decided to pay for it.

"Are you getting married soon?" the jeweler asked. "No." the young man answered. "I don't even have a girlfriend." The buyer was amused at the jeweler's dumb astonishment." "It's for my mother.", the young man said. "Before she gave birth, she was one her own. Someone told her to kill me before I was born, so as to avoid many problems. But she refused to do so, and she gave me the gift of life. And she had many troubles. She was a mother and a father to me; she was my friend, my sister and my teacher. Me brought me up to what I am, so now that I'm able to, I buy her this engagement ring. She never had one. I'll give it to her as a promise: if she did it all for me, now I will do it all for her. Maybe later I will give another engagement ring, but it will be the second one."

The jeweler said nothing. He only ordered his cashier to give the man a discount, which was only for important clients18.

Chapter Twelve

†

Touching the cloak of salvation

And there was a woman in the crowd who had had
a hemorrhage for twelve years. She had spent everything
she had on doctors and still could find no cure. She came up
behind Jesus and touched the fringe of his robe. Immediately,
the bleeding stopped. "Who touched me?" Jesus asked.
Everyone denied it, and Peter said, "Master, this whole crowd
is pressing up against you." But Jesus told him, "No, someone
deliberately touched me, for I felt healing power go out from me."
When the woman realized that Jesus knew, she began to
tremble and fell to her knees before him. The whole crowd
heard her explain why she had touched him and that she
had been immediately healed. "Daughter," he said to her,
"Your faith has made you well. Go in peace."
Luke 8:43-48 (See also Mattthew 9:20-22 and Mark 5:25-34)

Once upon a time, there was a group of boys quarreling at the school yard: "My father is much richer than yours, because he even has a new car" said one of the boys. "Oh! That's nothing!," said another one. "Mine is a thousand times richer than yours." "Richer?," asked the first boy. "Yes, my father even has a beautiful country house." "That's nothing," replied the third. "Nothing?" Asked the other two. "What does your father have?" So the third boy answered: "My father has faith in God and all we need he asks to Him, and so we have it."

Dear reader, what kind of God do you have? What kind of faith do you have? This passage tells us about a woman, who after many years of loss and suffering, came to Jesus and her problem was solved.

This story was very important to the heart and imagination of the primitive church. It was said that the woman was a gentil from Cesarea at Philippi. Eusebius, the great historian of the church in the third century, tells us that the woman had raised a statue with her own money, in memory of her healing, and that the statue remained there until Julian, the Roman emperor, trying to reestablish the pagan gods, destroyed it and built up his own in that same place, which was destroyed by a flash of lightning sent by God19.

This is just tradition, but the truth is that something happened to that woman. This story shows us four basic principles to bear in mind in order to understand better what God can do in our lives.

There was a woman in deep trouble

Mark says that, "She had suffered a great deal in the care of many doctors" and apart from spending all she had, she grew worse. Luke micht have not included this because he was a physician and he might have no liked this comment against his colleagues. The truth is that this woman, for twelve long years had been suffering from this illness, this disorder in her organism. Women, in particular, can understand perfectly this kind of problem. She had spent all her money and had not found a solution to it. I can personally understand this problem quite well, because my mother suffered from a similar disorder for many years, due to a bad surgery after my smaller brother was born. On many occasions, she was on the point of death and great part of the money that we had was spent on doctors, until, at last, someone could solve her problem. I remember that many times we thought as children that Mom would never come back home. We grew up thinking that at any moment, Mom could go with the Lord. Thanks to Him, He gave her many years of life and I can still have her, and she is the grandmother of many grandchildren.

You may be possibly in a similar situation, not that you may have a blood loss, but in the sence that you may have been losing your health, your money, your loved ones, your family or your spiritual life. It is possible that you may have tried it all to find a solution to your problem or the meaning of your life, such as sports, work, politics, religion, etc. but you have reached the conclusion that nothing and nobody and end so many years of loss. Let me remind you that God has different plans for each one of us, such as the Prophet Joel reminded the people of Israel (Joel 2:21-27).

The woman touched the edge of his cloak

This woman had lost it all, she had nothing to lose. Her last hope was before her eyes and she could not waste it; so she made her way through the crowd and she came up behind Jesus, she touched His cloak and she was immediately healed. She came up behind Him because of her shame, for, as William Barclay says, she was impure according to Jewish law. Her blood loss had steeled her life away; she was like a leper20. For that reason, she did not go openly to Jesus, but she dragged herself through the multitude, and that is why she felt ashamed and frightened when Jesus asked who had touched Him.

All the devout Jews wore tunics with fringed stripes, which ended in tassels of white linen with an interwoven blue thread. This reminded the Jew each time he dressed up or when he looked at them, that he was a son of God, who should carry out the law21. Scribes and Pharisees were very exaggerated in their clothes; this is why Jesus condemns them as hypocrite in another passage.

Years later, when it was dangerous to be a Jew, this tassels were worn in the underware. Nowadays, the Jews wear them in their talith or shawl with which they cover their head and shoulders while praying. But during Jesus' times, they were worn on the tunic22. Apparently, the woman touched one of those tassels.

Nowadays, many people are facing difficult situations, of which they may be ashamed, because these may be big or small in other people's eyes. They might have committed sins which might be shameful in human eyes;

but in this passage, we see that no matter the problem, God is always waiting for us with open arms.

As in the story of the prodigal son, Gods tells us now: "Come to my arms, give me your trouble. It doesn't matter if you come to me smelling of manure; it doesn't matter if you are heart broken; if you come on bare feet. Whatever your situation might be, come to me that I want to stretch you in my arms and tell you that I love you, that I want to forgive you, to help you. I want you to know that at the cross of Calvary, Jesus payed for all your offenses or sickness."

Jesus found out it was the woman

In spite of His disciples' excuses, Jesus knew that power had gone out from Him. Due to His insistence, knowing that she would not go unnoticed, the woman went trembling to Jesus and fell at His feet. In the presence of all people, she told the reason why she had touched Him and how she had been instantly healed.

It is wonderful that from the first moment when Jesus was face to face with the woman, there seemed to be nobody around. As Barclay says, they forgot about the multitude and Jesus spoke to the woman and treated her as if she was the only person in the world. The true love never thinks of people in terms of human importance23. True love makes a person feel loved even when a multitude is around. When God deals with us, His love is so big that He does it with great care and dedication, as if we were the only inhabitants of the planet.

A few days before the beginning of the Second World War, a woman was travelling by Georgia a she went to see an elderly woman who was very humble and poor and who lived in a cottage. The old country woman asked her if she was going to Moscow. The woman said she was. "Can you take some home made candies to my son? He can't get them in Moscow." Her son's name was Joseph Stalin. We do not normally think of the late Russian dictator as someone who would like home made candies, but his mother did. To her, the names men would give to him, had no importance24.

Almost all of us could have thought of the woman in the middle of the multitude as someone of no importance. To Jesus, she was someone who had a need and, thus, he left the multitude and gave Himself to her. This make us think that, in spite of the rest, in those moments God wants to treat us in a personal way. For this reason, we must leave our pride aside, our shame, our fears, our prejudices, the people's opinion and come to God to give Him our problem or, at least, to touch the edge of His cloak.

Jesus restored her completely

After that chat with the woman, he told her that her faith had healed her and that he could go in peace. She had come to Jesus with fear, ashamed, sick and from behind. Her encounter with Jesus not only healed her physically but also freed her completely. The woman gave her public testimony on what Jesus had done on her and she was completely restored. Now she could walk down the dusty streets of Israel with her head held high, with no fear and with no pain. She could start to save that money she would have spent on doctors. It was all in the past, for as the Gospel says: "If someone is in Christ, he is a new creature; the old things have passed, Gods makes them all new."

When we experience a blessing from God, He wants us to tell others about it so as to encourage their faith and for His glory. But He also wants us to walk our Christian life in freedom, with our head up high and with an abundant life. A true encounter with Jesus gives us all that and even more.

What is your father like? My heavenly father is the most richest in abundant grace, mercy and forgiveness. Nowadays we find many people who, as that woman, are losing in different areas of their lives, people to whom the devil is taking away the riches that God has to give them. We need to allow that Jesus touches us, that He closes the doors where we are losing his riches, that he stops the bleeding through which we are losing our life, our faith, our strength, our health or our financial welfare.

As it was told, a newly converted man who was always coming back to his old sins, went on repeating: "Lord, fill me with your grace, fill me with your Holy Spirit, fill me with everything, My Lord." Once he finished praying, a brother who knew him well got up and began to pray: "Oh!, Lord, don't fill him again. He's full of leaks and he loses all the grace You give him. I ask you to repair his leaks first."

If there are leaks in our lives, God expects us that we get close to Him. He wishes to repair everything that make us lose and He wants to fill us again.

Study guide

Introduction

Summarize the story of the children who argued over whose father was the richest.

Transitional phrase

What kind of God do we have, what kind of faith do we profess? This story is the testimony of a woman, who after many years of loss, came to Jesus and her problem was solved.

Bible reading

Luke 8:43-48, Matthew 9:20-22 and Mark 5:25-34

In this story we find four basic elements that we must bear in mind so as to understand better what Jesus can make in our lives.

1. There was a woman with a serious problem

For twelve years this woman had send all she had on physicians and she got worse. Nowadays there are people who have possibly tried everything to solve their problem with no success.

2. The woman touched the edge of Jesus'cloak

She had lost everything, she had nothing to lose now. She came from behind and touched Jesus' cloak. It doesn't matter if our problems are big or small, in Christ we find the possiblility of solving them.

3. Jesus found out it was the woman

In the middle of the crowd, Jesus saw a woman in need. For God we are not numbers; He treat us like individuals and know exactly what we need.

4. Jesus restored her completely

Jesus not only healed her physically, but also He restored her spiritually. She gave her public testimony on what Jesus did for her and she was completely freed.

Conclusion

What is our Heavenly Father like? Maybe you have been losing for a while, but now God wants to heal your wounds, restore your faith or family. Turn to Jesus and experiment all that He has for you. Allow that God fill your leaks that make you lose your blessings.

Questions for study and discussion

1. Where was Jesus going when this happened?

2. What was the problem of this woman?

3. How was a woman in her condition seen by her community?

4. Which other resources had this woman tried and how did it work out?

5. Why did she came to Jesus from behind?

6. What happened after she touched Jesus' cloak?

7. How and why did Jesus react in that way?

8. Which was Jesus' answer after the woman confessed what had happened?

9. What was the woman's response to Jesus' insistence?

10. Which was the miracle that was performed in her life?

Applicational activities

1. Which situations of loss have you been through or are you through at this moment?

2. Which resourses have you tried to solve them and how did it work out?

3. Have you ever tried turning to Jesus? If the answer is yes, say how did it work out and if the answer is no, turn to Jesus now.

4. Which is the idea you have on God and what kind of faith do you profess?

Appetizer for the Soul XIII

✝

The Chinese quarry worker

There was once a small Chinese man, who was very happy with his job: breaking up stone in a quarry. Until one day, he saw the caravan of a great Oriental King coming with all his subjects who followed and served him. He sat on an enormous elephant, under a golden canopy.

He was so amazed at all this magnificence, that he wished to be someone else and to do something else; and he wished it so fervently that, at that moment, he turned into a great Oriental king. He was travelling with his subjects who served him. His ministers and army officers bowed at his command till they touched the floor. One very hot day, they made a real effort to calm his thirst, but it was useless because the sun was at its peak. Feeling hot and tired, he looked above and thought that the sun was more powerful than him.

So once again, he made a wish: he wanted to become the sun. At that moment he became the sun and he was so hot and strong that men were out of breath. The grass was burned and the earth cracked. He made some people die of thirst, his influence was such that he felt powerful and happy. Until, all of a sudden, a thick black cloud got in his way. The sun was strong, but no matter how much he tried, his rays would not reach the earth. He looked at the black cloud and he realized that it was more powerful than him.

So once again, he made a wish: this time he wanted to become a cloud. He became a cloud and as he went from one place to another he caused floods and damage; with his lightning he chopped down trees and caused fires. He felt much more powerful than the sun, until one day he found a crag. Though he tried really hard, he could do nothing to it, because it was solid rock. Tired and exhausted, he realized that the crag was more powerful than him.

So now he wished to become a crag. And he turned into solid rock. Now he was satisfied, proud and he felt powerful. Neither the sun nor the cloud could harm him. He was implacable, as we want to be many times: that nothing and nobody can harm us.

Until one day, "Oh! Ouch!", he screamed. " What's happening?" he asked. There was a man on his back who was breaking up the stone.

Once again, he wished to be what he had been once: a little quarry worker, and he never wished again to become or do something else. And he lived happily everafter.

We live wishing to be someone else, feeling envy on what we do not have, on someone else's boyfriend, property, intelligence, etc; and for this reason, we are often unhappy and we no not realize that we cannot be what we are meant to, nor do what God wants us to. He has made us original, unique and that is exactly what we should be, instead of a cheap copy or a poor imitation. He wishes us to walk with Him using all the resources He has given us, and to be conformed to the likeness of our Lord Jesus Christ (Romans 8:29)25.

Chapter Thirteen

✝

Feeding many with little

When the apostles returned, they told Jesus everithing they
had done. Then he slipped quietly away with them toward
the town of Bethsaida. But the crowds found out where he
was going, and they followed him. And he welcomed them,
teaching them about the Kingdom of God and curing those
who were hill. Late in the afternoon the twelve disciples came
to him and said, "Send the crowds away to the nearby villages
and farms, so they can find food and lodging for the night.
There is nothing to eat here in this desert place." But Jesus
said, "You feed them." "Imposible!" they protested." We
have only five loaves of bread and two fish. Or are you
expecting us to go and buy enough food for this whole
crowd? For there were about five thousand men there.
"Just tell them to sit down on the ground in groups of about
fifty each," Jesus replied. So the people all sat down. Jesus
took the five loaves and two fish, looked up toward heaven,
and asked God's blessing on the food. Breaking the loaves
into pieces, he kept giving the bread and fish to the disciples
to give to the people. They all at as much as they wanted,
and they picked up twelve baskets of leftovers!
Luke 9:10-17 (See also Matthew 14:13-21; Mark 6:32-44 and Jn 6:5-13)

This passage tells us about the enormous responsibility that we have as a church to proclaim the good news of the Gospel. Many people ask themselves: "Where is God when people suffer?" Indeed, the more suitable question should be: "Where is the church when people suffer?" God delayed His authority and responsibility on His church and we are the extension of his hands and feet. Jesus has no plan B to let the world know what He has done for humanity. The church is his only plan; therefore we must assume such responsibility. A transforming experience with Jesus makes our hearts burdened with those who do not know Jesus and who need Him.

This story is the only miracle that has been registered in the four Gospels; its main point is to make us see that Jesus is also the Lord of material things. Jesus saw a great multitude who was in need and He did something out of a few things that came to His hands. We need to understand that if, as a church or as individuals, we want to act specifically on human needs, we need to present our lives, gifts, talents, skills, resources to God so that He may take them and bless them.

This miracle occurred probably on April of the year 29 AD., that is, about a year before Jesus' death. He had previously been to Jerusalem and now, with His disciples, he went to the other side of the sea of Galilee, According to the Gospels it was near Bethsaida Julia, a new city built by Philip the Tetrarch. In Hebrew, Bethsaida means "house of fish" in honor of the sea of Galilee, due to its great quantity of fish and "Julia" in the honor of the beautiful daughter of the emperor August, who had died26.

Jesus and His disciples wanted to go to a quiet and solitary place, for His disciples had come back from a missionary trip and they needed to be alone to evaluate it. Moreover, Jesus had recently heard the news of John the Baptist's death. So they chose a quiet place to meditate and assess the last events.

As they saw Jesus on board ready to cross the sea, the people walked down the shore to where He and His disciples were. But they did not go to Him because they recognized Him as their Lord and Savior but because they were greatly impressed by His miracles. Actually, these were only signals, but the multitude did not understand it and they expected their Messiah to be a political figure.

According to history, it's spring in Israel in the month of April; thus, it's no surprise that Jesus wanted to spend a day in the open air, which was fresh and pure, in contact with nature and with His disciples on that green hill, covered by irises and under a blue sky and a radiant sun.

The four Gospels give us many details only to show prove the authenticity of the event. This story gives us some principles which we should bear in mind if we want to be a means of blessing to others.

We must see the multitude in need

As the saying goes: "There is no one so blind as those that will not see." From the hill top, Jesus could easily see the multitude that was getting near; but far from considering them as a nuisance, He came down the hill because, as Mathew says, He felt "compassion on them". In a way, we as Christians find ourselves on a spiritual hill from where we can see reality and the true needs in our society. There are real needs, if we don't want to see them, that's another story. If we are not able to feel compassion for the lost ones, our message will never have the passion and urgency with which it should be delivered. Jude 23 says: "snatch others from the fire and save them". We must forget about ourselves for a minute and think about others. We need to stop being a centripetal church to turn into a centrifugal community.

We must worry for real facts

Time elapsed quickly, the evening was near as also the first shadows of the night. The day had been long but productive. The day had been long. Many miracles and healings had been performed. Then His disciples came to Him and said: "This is a remote place, and it's already getting late. Send the crowds away, so that they can go to the villages and buy themselves some food." But Jesus said, "You feed them."

How many times, as Christians and as the church of Christ, do we do the same? We see the needy, but we dismiss them without giving them any help, because we think of us. But it is our responsibility to satisfy the needs of others; and we must do so through real acts of love. Many times people wonder, even Christians: "Where is God when there are people suffering from all kind of needs?" But I believe that this question must go in the opposite direction, the right question should be: Where is the church when the people is suffering?" God has entrusted us, He commended us to do what He did during his ministry on earth.

Dangers of a merely human view

Facing God's challenge to supply for the needs of our neighbor, in general, we have a very human vision on the circumstances. The disciples contemplated the enormous multitude and immediately they took out their own speculations; they charged all the information on their data base and got to the conclusion that the only they had were five loaves of bread and two fish, that according to John, a boy had given to them, and which were made of barley.

In those days, barley bread was the one that the poor ate, the white bread was more expensive. Nowadays is exactly the opposite. When the disciples saw those loaves of bread and the two fish they exclaimed: "Only five loaves of bread and two fish! What is this for so many! I suppose that the disciples must have got desperate. They only saw five loaves of bread and two fish and , on the other side, the immense crowd; but they did not see or think of Jesus, of His power and His love. In those moments, the attitude of little faith characterized them all.

How many times do we do the same? We see the needs, we see the small resources and we say: "It's not enough!" So we stay with our arms crossed, doing nothing and we forget to look at Jesus. In general, we give more credit to difficulties than to Jesus. Someone said: "The more we think about God's goodness, the less we worry about the needs around us." This is what we call the locust way of thinking. As the ten spies that went to see the land to conquer, we see the walls and the gigants, but we forget about the power of God. With God, as a well known song says, "we can jump over the walls".

Divine strategy

Jesus does not reproach them their lack of faith, but He encourages them to sit all the people in groups of fifty and a hundred persons. There was a total of five thousand men, without counting the women and the children, which could easily be twice the number of men.

Now, let's use our imagination: there were fifteen thousand people with their colorful dresses, sitting in groups of fifty and a hundred people on the green grass, at the foot of the hill covered in irises of many colors. The sun was setting over the sea of Galilee and on the background there were many colors like gold, red, orange, yellow. It was really like a sapphire among a field of emeralds. Did these people expect a miracle? Of course they did, for they obeyed immediately the order to sit down in groups of fifty and a hundred each.

This was Jesus' strategy: to gather them in cells so that no one would remain with no food. This teach us that, today, as a church, we need to organize ourselves to reach all the persons and to supply for their needs. With no strategies or goals we may be wasting our resources or giving more to one group and less to another.

Divine vision

Strategies and goals are good, but they should never restrict God's power or His vision on things. On verse 16 we find the simple narration on the miracle. It says: "Taking the five loaves and the two fish and looking up to heaven, He gave thanks and broke them. Then He gave them to the disciples to set before the people." Here is the key to a divine vision, to a right vision.

According to the Gospel, they were five loaves of barley bread and two fish. So little for so many! But Jesus did not reject them. God specializes Himself in doing great things with a few resources. He fed Elisha on the little flour and oil of a widow. He defeated an army of twenty thousand soldiers with a group of three hundred; he tore down the walls of Jerico with a couple of shouts. The Bible is full of magnificent stories of God, outstanding in His power and greatness. Now this is a similar case. Jesus did not reject those few loaves of bread and those fish; He neither complained over the fact that the bread was low quality. On the contrary, The Bible says that Jesus took those loaves and those fish, He blessed them and then He gave them to His disciples so that they would set them before the people. We do not know when the multiplication miracle happened, what we do know is that everybody ate what they wanted and there was still food left.

On many occasions, we excuse ourselves before God that we do not have many gifts, or skills or economical resourses, or that our service or our contribution is insignificant and, thus, the years go by and we do nothing. But in these days, God challenges us to bring to Jesus all we have, little or a lot. If we give it to Him; He will take us in His arms, He will bless us and we will be protagonists of the miracle that God wants to perform among us. We must start, we must put our feet in the Jordan and God will do the rest.

As a Church, our responsibility is to satisfy the people's needs; but if in our lives, our gifts, skills or resources are not blessed by God, it will be no use to try to do anything. Our responsibility is to cooperate and not to compete.

The barley bread remained being barley bread; it was multiplied but not changed. As a result from this miracle, five important things took place:

- They were all satisfied.

- There was food left.

- There was admiration for Jesus.

- They tried to make Jesus their king.

- Jesus went to the hill to pray and to be alone.

If we accept the challenge to carry out our mission as a church, with the vision of heaven, taht is, with our lives, gifts, talents and resourses blessed by Jesus, then we will also witness the results, for instance:

· People will find a response to their needs and they will become believers.

· There will be plenty of resources, both economical as spiritual, that we must not waste but administer correctly. The fact that there are unlimited resources is no excuse to abuse them.

· People will talk about the church, they will comment on what is happening, there will be admiration and criticism.

· People will want to use the Lord to meet their own needs, as they wanted to do at that moment and during all the ministry of Jesus. They search for the bread and the fish but not to the one who gives them.

· On many occasions we will need, as a Church and individually, to retire from popularity to meditate alone with our Father.

The time of Jesus' coming is near. We have a great and hard task to carry out. No one else will do our job. Jesus has no other plan. But with Him as the head and together as a body, not even the gates of hell will prevail against us. It is time for the denominational barriers to fall, it is time to build up a church with no walls.

Outside the walls of our buildings, there is an immense multitude that we must serve. We need to feel compassion for them and to compromise with our deeds. Jesus' call from the cross "I'm thirsty" is still echoing from eternity in thousands of millions of people who are thirsty and hungry of the water and the bread of life, of the true bread and the true water that is Jesus, the only one who can fulfill such need. We must do some speculations and we must develop our strategies, but we must not minimize God's power. It is necessary that we dig the grain of wheat so that it may die and bear much fruit; that is, we need to deny ourselves and allow that

God takes us, bless us and multiply us. It is time that we dedicate once again our lives to Jesus so that we become protagonists to reap the final harvest, because the fields are ready for the harvest.

Study guide
Introduction

Church is the only plan Jesus has created to take the good news to the lost people and all our contribution, even if it is small, blessed by Him can have miraculous results.

Transitional phrase

This passage in the Bible will show us how a few resources in God's hands satisfied the hunger of many people.

Lectura bíblica Bible reading

Luke 9:10-17; Mathew 14: 13-21; Mark 6:32-44 and John 6:5-13

This is the only miracle told in the four Gospels, it presents many principles that we must bear in mind if we want to be means of blessing to others.

1. We must see the multitude in need

Needs are real and they do exist. We must forget about ourselves and look around.

2. We compromise in deed

The disciples wanted to dismiss the hungry multitude, but Jesus challenged them to feed them. Today's challenge is still the same for us.

3. Dangers of a merely human vision

In general, we have a human vision of things, as the disciples, who contemplated the multitude and their few resources.

4. Divine strategy

Jesus does not complain about their lack of faith, but He orders them to divide the multitude into groups. In this passage, Jesus teaches us to be organized and to think of a strategy to reach them. Without strategies we may waste our resources.

5. Divine vision

Strategies are good, but we cannot minimize God's power. Jesus did not see just a few loaves and fish. He saw what God would do with them. If our lives, gifts, talents, resouces are blessed by Jesus, miracles will be performed.

Conclusion

As there were many results in this story, in the same way, live dedicated to God, walking in God's vision, will produce great results for the glory of God. Outside there is a great multitude that is hungry and thirsty of the water and the bread of life, of Jesus. We are responsible, as His church, to fulfill that need.

Questions for study and discussion

1. Where did the apostles come back from and on what did they report to Jesus?

2. Why did Jesus withdrew His disciples?

3. Where was located Bethsaida?

4. What did the people do when they saw Jesus and His disciples sailing to the other side?

5. What did Jesus do with the multitude that had come to them?

6. What did the disciples suggested Jesus at the end of the day?

7. What did Jesus suggest His disciples?

8. What was Jesus' strategy?

9. Which were Jesus' resources and what did He do with the loaves of bread and the fish?

10. Which were the results of that miracle? Name five at least.

Applicational activities

1. Which is the challenge your are facing?

2. Which has been your excuse until now?

3. Which are the resourses you count on now?

4. What are you going to do with them?

5. Which is the miracle that you can visualize? Leave a space in your heart and mind so that God may surprise you.

Conclusion

We have come to the end of the first part of transforming encounters with Jesus, according to Luke's Gospel. As we said in the introduction of this book, we have gone through thirteen of these encounters and there are many left. Each story had its own special characteristics; some of them may have touched us personally in a deeper way, some others may have been a blessing to other people.

Who has never felt rejected or of small value to others? For those, there is hope in Jesus, because He specializes in calling the undesirables to His kingdom.

Who has never thought that his sin or situation was impossible to forgive or solve? For those, there is hope in Jesus, for He specializes in touching the untouchable.

Who has never had any doubts as to the divinity of Jesus? Welcome to the clan! Jesus is still God whether or not we question His divinity or His goodness. He is ready to prove that He really is God. He does not need our defense.

Who has never been paralysed facing a difficult situation? The good news is that Jesus specializes in setting in motion what is paralysed, what has been still or with no use.

Who has never been surprised by bad news while on vacations? Jesus specializes in helping us to endure those unpleasant moments.

Who has never been through the loss of something or someone he loved very much? Jesus specializes in giving us hope in despair, commfort in pain, life in death. He specializes in changing our funeral procession into a joyful walk.

Who has never been in a moment of deep dissatisfaction? Jesus is the special treasure and He wants us all to be ready to leave the good to be filled with the best.

Who has never felt like the people of Israel before the gigant Goliath? Jesus specializes in making His sons conquerors of the evil hosts, even when it means to face Satan and His whole army.

Who has never been submerged in the depths of anxiety and depression? Jesus is a specialist in taking us out of such estate, in changing our lament into dance and in changing the human diagnosis.

Who has never turned to Jesus as a last resource? His grace is still available for those who need to be healed and saved even if they look for him covertly.

Who has never faced a challenge with few resources or even none? Jesus is the champion in transforming the little we may have to offer into a means of blessing to multitudes.

There are stories of men and women that have made a great impact on Christianism for centuries. Many of those stories are worth telling and I believe that they are the sequel to the book of Acts of the Apostles, which would be most appropriate to call Acts of the Holy Spirit. But it is also truth that, on many occasions, we lose the blessing of hearing old stories, like the ones in the Gospel, because we are craving to hear something new.

This book has the objective of taking us back to our roots and rediscover or revalue the precious pearls they have to bless our lives. Before I finish, allow me to make some suggestions. First, if it has been of help in your life, recommend it to other people. Second, use this material as a study guide at home. You can invite your relatives, neighbors, friends, fellow workers or students and you may study together each one of these passages. The brief stories titled "Peaceful thoughts" can be used as an incentive to start or finish those study meetings at home. If you have never had a study meeting at home, talk to your pastor, offer him your house and offer yourself as a leader to that group. For a moment, just think of how many people you many impact as time goes by. If you think you can't do that, study over and over again the last chapter of this book, and you will see that you have no excuses. The value of our lives is not measured for what we have accumulated, but by how many lives have we impacted on.

I bless your life in this pilgrimage and I share the joy of the fruits you may produce for the extension and the strengthening of God's kingdom.

Yours in Christ,

Enrique

Bibliography

✝

Barclay, William. *Lucas*. Argentina, La Aurora, 1973, 290 pp.

Biblia: La Biblia de las Amércias. Estados Unidos, Editorial Fundación, 1986

Douglas, J. D. *Nuevo Diccionario Bíblico*. Colombia, Certeza, 1991,1479 pp.

Holy Bible: New Living Translation. Tyndale House Publishers, Inc. Wheaton, Illinois, 1996.

Footnotes

1 Message received from: w.larralde@symnetics.com.ar

2 Message received from: BocaRiver@distantshore.com

3 Message received from: w.larralde@symnetics.com.ar

4 Menssage received from: hugjesilv@sion.com

5 Message received from: w.larralde@symnetics.com.ar

6 William Barclay. *Lucas*. Argentina, Ediciones La Aurora, 1983, pg. 66

7 William Barclay. *Lucas*. Argentina, Ediciones La Aurora, 1983, pg. 66

8 William Barclay. *Lucas*. Argentina, Ediciones La Aurora, 1983, pg. 66

9 Message received from: w.larralde@symnetics.com.ar

10 Message received from: gorito85@elsitio.com

11 Message received from: BocaRiver@distantshore.com

12 William Barclay. *Lucas*. Argentina, Ediciones La Aurora, 1983, pg. 88

13 William Barclay. *Lucas*. Argentina, Ediciones La Aurora, 1983, pg. 88

14 William Barclay. *Lucas*. Argentina, Ediciones La Aurora, 1983, pg. 89

15 Message received from: bernabei@sion.com

16 Message received from: RossanaF@hilsea.com.ec

17 Message received from: sgulisan@ta.telecom.com.ar

18 Menssage received from: bernabei@sion.com

19 William Barclay. *Luke*. Argentina, Ediciones La Aurora, 1983, pg. 112

20 William Barclay. *Luke*. Argentina, Ediciones La Aurora, 1983, pg. 112

21 William Barclay. *Luke*. Argentina, Ediciones La Aurora, 1983, pg. 112

22 William Barclay. *Luke*. Argentina, Ediciones La Aurora, 1983, pg. 112

23 William Barclay. *Luke*. Argentina, Ediciones La Aurora, 1983, pg. 112

24 William Barclay. *Luke*. Argentina, Ediciones La Aurora, 1983, pg. 113

25 Menssage received from: bernabei@sion.com

26 J. D. Douglas. *Nuevo Diccionarioo Bíblico*. Colombia, Certeza, 1991, pg. 180

This book finished printing on April, 2005
in DOCUPRINT S.A.
Rivadavia 701 (1002) Buenos Aires,
Argentina
www.docuprint.com